T0359225

Essential Text Types

A Writing Guide for Students

Diane White and Elli Housden

NELSON
CENGAGE Learning

Australia • Brazil • Japan • Korea • Mexico • Singapore • Spain • United Kingdom • United States

NELSON
CENGAGE Learning

Essential Text Types
1st Edition
Diane White
Elli Housden

Cover designer: Book Design Ltd
Text designer: Belinda Davis and Book Design Ltd
Production controller: Siew Han Ong

Any URLs contained in this publication were checked
for currency during the production process. Note,
however, that the publisher cannot vouch for the
ongoing currency of URLs.

For product information and technology assistance,
in Australia call 1300 790 853;
in New Zealand call 0800 449 725

For permission to use material from this text or product, please email
aust.permissions@cengage.com

National Library of New Zealand Cataloguing-in-Publication Data
A catalogue record for this book is available from the National Library
of New Zealand.

ISBN: 978 0 17025741 1

Cengage Learning Australia
Level 7, 80 Dorcas Street
South Melbourne, Victoria Australia 3205

Cengage Learning New Zealand
Unit 4B Rosedale Office Park
331 Rosedale Road, Albany, North Shore 0632, NZ

For learning solutions, visit cengage.co.nz

Printed in Australia by Ligare Pty Limited.
2 3 4 5 6 7 8 20 19 18 17 16

Introduction

Students in New Zealand schools in English classrooms are expected to write. At NCEA Levels 1, 2 and 3 they are expected to write in a variety of genres, with purpose, control and effectiveness. They are expected to write accurately, observing conventions of structure and grammar.

Essential Text Types intends to provide examples of writing in a wide variety of text types, allowing students to observe the professional and student writer in practice. The examples provided will help students to understand what is expected of them when they themselves are asked to write.

Suggestions for student writing exercises have been included and key terms are listed in a glossary.

All of the text types are presented in a double-page format allowing the student to observe the example provided to support the generic structure that this guide outlines.

When students begin a piece of writing it helps if they have some idea of *why* they are writing, *what* they are hoping to achieve by writing, and *for whom* they are writing before putting pen to paper, or fingers to keyboard.

Often when they read, these essentials are not considered. This guide is intended to present the *intentions* of a type of writing first and an *example* to demonstrate how a writer achieves those intentions.

Contents

Appendix

1. Definition:

An **advertisement** is a text that attempts to sell a product or a service.

2. Purpose and Role of Writer:

to promote, to persuade someone to buy a product or service

3. Generic Features:

a) Structure and Organisation

- eye-catching layout that 'jumps off the page'
- uncluttered and simple for clarity
- a mixture of written and visual text, bold and balanced
- focus on originality and readability; large bold print
- interesting font, contemporary and fashionable illustration

b) Language

- clear, accurate information to facilitate ease of purchase
- persuasive or emotive language e.g. *safe; sensible; help; revitalised*
- text to suit product e.g. *natural active ingredients*
- text to suit audience / potential buyer's tastes and needs e.g. *problem skin conditions; harakeke*
- may use statistics, relevant terminology, humour, testimonials, rhyme, alliteration, puns, exaggeration, repetition of keywords to reinforce an image e.g. *'more than 100' statistic; repetition of 'free'*

c) Grammar

- effective adjectives e.g. *natural; sensitive; dry; cracked*
- effective verbs e.g. *cares; help relieve; soothe*
- second person pronoun e.g. *your*
- imperative e.g. *ENJOY*
- present tense e.g. *it works, it's natural*

made right here in New Zealand

A natural range of skincare for dry and sensitive skin that actually works!

It's natural:
Safe, sensible skincare with New Zealand sourced manuka honey and harakeke flax that cares for your skin and our planet. Safe for all skin types.

It Works:
DermaLab will leave your skin feeling revitalised and will help relieve problem skin conditions like acne, eczema, sensitive dry and cracked skin.

Dermatological Formulation:
Developed in conjunction with dermatologists and more than 100 New Zealand families to soothe problem skin. Your skin will look and feel revitalised when you use DermaLab which is packed with natural active ingredients.

DermaLab
it's natural and it works

Available at leading pharmacies.
www.dermalab.co.nz

DermaLab
it's natural and it works

01. gentle cleansing
natural body and face wash with new zealand manuka honey and colloidal oatmeal.
for dry and sensitive skin.

HYPOALLERGENIC:
Dermatological Formulation

DermaLab is packed with natural active ingredients using the best of nature and science. When we say natural we mean natural - so we won't use parabens, artificial colours or fragrances. It's natural and it works - ENJOY!

Made in New Zealand   430ml

Hypoallergenic • Fragrance Free • Skin Friendly pH • Colour Free • Paraben Free

Annotations:
- contemporary, less formal font
- visual balance
- persuasive language
  Maori words for NZ audience
  ecologically attractive words
- scientific words
- practical information
- reflection in water/snow suggests clean, pure
- repetition

1. Definition:

An **agenda** is a programme of business to be undertaken at a meeting. It is presided over by a chairperson.

Minutes are the written notes taken at a meeting by the secretary. These record what was discussed at the meeting for future reference and serve as a historical and legal record of the proceedings. Minutes are a nonfiction text.

2. Purpose and Role of Writer:

to record information precisely and accurately, usually by the secretary of the organisation

3. Generic Features:

a) Structure and Organisation

- prescribed format and headings e.g. *Agenda; Minutes; Present; Apologies*
- numbered list format for business to be discussed
- may be a concise summary or word for word transcript

b) Language

- specific language associated with meetings e.g. *Chair; Matters arising; Other business; Minutes*
- clear, concise, factual language and easy to read
- may require accurate transcription of spoken language
- may include quotations from participants

c) Grammar

- sentences and paragraphs
- sentence fragments e.g. *moved*
- past tense e.g. *opened; reported*; future tense e.g. *Joe Crowley will*
- third person / impersonal, e.g. he, they
- accurate spelling of names and terms

**Agenda of the North West Football Club Committee Meeting
1 October 2015**

1. Minutes of the last meeting
2. Matters arising   ·· prescribed format and
3. Reports: terminology
    - Treasurer
    - Director of Coaching
4. Other business

**Minutes of the North West Football Club Committee Meeting
held at the North West Football Clubhouse 1 October 2015**

The meeting opened at 7 p.m.   ·················· prescribed format and
                                                terminology

Chair: Matthew Jones

Present: Jim Anderson, Nathan Bell, Liam Connors,
Andrew Dent and Eddie Edwards

Apologies: Sandy Simpson, Joe Crowley ·············· accuracy

Minutes of the Previous Meeting: moved J. Anderson,
seconded N. Bell that the minutes of the September meeting
be accepted as a true and accurate record.

Business Arising from the Minutes:
- Jim Anderson is to organise transport to next month's game
  at New Plymouth.
- Eddie Edwards is to assist the Secretary for the rest of
  the year.   ·············· concise factual language

Treasurer's Report: moved L. Connors, seconded A. Dent
that the financial report be accepted.

Director of Coaching Report: reported on injuries so far
this season and fitness strategies for the rest of the season.
Moved E. Edwards, seconded N. Bell that the coaching report
be accepted.   ·············· language is businesslike,
                                                       formal

Other business:
- Sandy Simpson has agreed to organise the Christmas party.
- Joe Crowley will purchase the new footballs for next season. ········ future tense

The Chair closed the meeting at 9.10 p.m. ·············· past tense

Next Meeting: 3 November 2015 ·············· conclusion

1. Definition:

An **autobiography** is the story of a person's life as told by that person. Some people use a 'ghost writer' to help them write their own story.

A **biography** is the story of a person's life written by another person.

Autobiographies / biographies are usually written by / about prominent people and their life experiences and achievements. Unauthorised biographies are written without the permission of the person whose life is being described. Often the author of the biography is not acquainted with the person featured in his or her book.

A **memoir** is a piece of autobiographical writing, usually shorter than a comprehensive autobiography. A memoir often tries to capture certain moments or particular events in a person's past, rather than documenting every fact of his or her life, and may be more emotional than a complete autobiography.

2. Purpose and Role of Writer:

to tell an interesting story; to inform or reveal details about a person's life for historical or personal reasons, or for profit

3. Generic Features:

a) Structure and Organisation

- book format; divided into chapters
- arrangement may be chronological or thematic, e.g. early years, schooldays, successes, failures
- content outlines significant events from the person's life, e.g. rites of passage
- may include personal or relevant photographs, pictures, illustrations

b) Language

- autobiography: personal; reflecting author's personality e.g. *I was on cloud nine*
- biography: a degree of formality creates some distance between writer and reader
  e.g. *John Lennon was arguably the genius*
- autobiography and memoir: subjective; influenced by the opinion of the author
  e.g. *I expected the manager to evict him immediately*
- biography: generally factual and objective, depending on the writer's purpose. If the author wishes to influence the reader, he or she may use subjective language or select facts to suit the purpose. e.g. *he had humble beginnings*
- writing style: engages the reader through description and brings the subject to life
  e.g. dialogue: *'Just this once,' Bob growled*

c) Grammar

- accurate English in complete sentences
- first person for autobiography and memoir; third person for biography
  e.g. *when I was famous; John was born in Liverpool*
- past tense is more common because of content e.g. *The Beatles were the music phenomenon*

An extract from *The Autobiography of a Rock Star*

I'll never forget my first gig. I was convinced at the time it would be my last.

first person / conversational style / addresses audience

A new club had opened in town so I got a job there as a bar attendant. I'd worked all over the country serving drinks in the last few years, trying to break into the music scene. So I was an ace cocktail shaker.

references to personal things / personal opinions / subjective comments

After a couple of weeks, I finally convinced my manager to let me have a place in the Saturday evening music line-up.

'Just this once,' Bob growled, 'because I'm short of solo performers. But don't expect it to become a habit. And if you're really awful, you'll be off that stage after the first bar.'

dialogue creates authenticity and variety

Well, when the evening came, I got through the first song no worries. I was on cloud nine by the time the audience had finished clapping. And then a little nondescript man stood up in the audience. He'd had a bit to drink, I think. 'That's my song,' he insisted, and climbed onto the stage.

development of story / descriptive style

I expected the manager to evict him immediately. But, wouldn't you know it? Bob was an old fan of this 'has been'. And the old boy could sing. It was back behind the bar for me.

story takes a negative turn

'Stick to cocktails,' I was told. I quit the job that night.

Years later, when I was famous, I ran into Bob. He apologised and he asked for my autograph.

conclusion reveals theme of story and ironic ending

An extract from *A Biography of John Lennon*

The Beatles were the music phenomenon of the twentieth century. And John Lennon was arguably the genius of the band, with his prolific song-writing talents. Yet he had humble beginnings and his future did not look promising.

impersonal style / reader is distanced from writer / writer expresses personal opinion

John was born in Liverpool in 1940. His parents, who were both quite musical, separated early in his life and he was brought up by an aunt and uncle. It seemed that he was destined for a career in art, before he discovered music. Although he failed his final high school exams narrowly, Lennon was admitted to the Liverpool Art College. Here he met his first wife, Cynthia. Disruptive in class, he left art school a year before finishing the course.

factual detail / emotionally detached from subject and audience

It was his mother, Julia, who gave Lennon his first guitar. While still at high school, he formed his first band, The Quarrymen. He attracted Paul McCartney and later George Harrison to the group. For this reason, John Lennon is widely regarded as the first Beatle.

conclusion maintains formal tone with some opinionative comment / writer's personality is not revealed

1. Definition:

A **brochure** is a small booklet or folded piece of A4 paper, designed for informational and promotional purposes.

A **flyer** is a single-page advertisement or handbill.

2. Purpose and Role of Writer:

to inform and persuade; to 'sell' an idea or a service

3. Generic Features:

a) Structure and Organisation

- divided into small logical sections according to subject and purpose
- information organised into smaller subtexts for easier interpretation
- eye-catching layout
- front cover should make purpose explicit
- inside pages should contain more detailed text
- some use of visual text e.g. maps / illustrations
- attractive illustration; variety of fonts to create visual appeal

b) Language

- clear and concise language e.g. *is in the open sea*
- persuasive language e.g. *eco-tourism adventure*
- informative language e.g. *only 80km north of Auckland*
- language to suit product or purpose e.g. *underwater world; marine life*
- factual and persuasive words e.g. *NO FISH NO CHARGE*
- language to appeal to target group/s e.g. *exciting and educational*

c) Grammar

- short sentences / fragments e.g. *Duration – 45 mins*
- imperatives e.g. *For bookings call; Peer into*
- present tense e.g. *we offer; gives different views*
- second person pronoun e.g. *your* and / or inclusive pronouns e.g. *we; us*

We offer an exciting and educational experience for all ages

GOAT ISLAND NZ
GLASS BOTTOM BOAT TOURS

Peer into the marine life of New Zealand's natural underwater world at Goat Island Marine reserve

BOOKINGS ESSENTIAL

ONLY 80KM NORTH OF AUCKLAND, NEAR LEIGH
(APPROX. 1 HOURS DRIVE)

EACH BOAT TOUR IS UNIQUE

AROUND THE ISLAND FULL COMMENTARY CRUISING TOUR

Departs from Goat Island Marine Reserve Beach
Duration - 45 mins | Check in time 30 mins prior to departure

This eco-tourism adventure gives different views of the many varied fish and natural marine life both above and below the water.

$28. per adult | $15. per child (3 to 15 yrs)
Discount prices available for schools and larger groups by arrangement.

GOAT ISLAND NZ
GLASS BOTTOM BOAT TOURS

09 422 6334 or 0274 979 764
info@glassbottomboat.co.nz | www.glassbottomboat.co.nz

WE GUARANTEE - NO FISH NO CHARGE

Goat Island Marine Reserve is in the open sea, so please understand that sometimes tours can be cancelled due to bad weather or poor water clarity.

Bookings and confirmation of the sea conditions are advised.

To avoid disappointment, please call us to check sea and wind conditions before leaving your base.

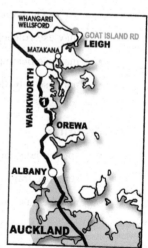

BOOK ONLINE AT
www.glassbottomboat.co.nz
OR CALL 09 4226334

To avoid disappointment, please call us to check sea and wind conditions before leaving your base

GOAT ISLAND MARINE RESERVE
GOAT ISLAND ROAD, GOAT ISLAND, LEIGH

Brochure / Flyer ISBN: 9780170355568 • 13

1. Definition:

A **documentary** is a film that attempts to document reality, or a nonfiction film based on factual or real-life events.

2. Purpose and Role of Writer:

to inform and comment on an event or issue

3. Generic Features:

a) Structure and Organisation

- may be chronological, or based on aspects of an event or issue
- divided into scenes / camerawork may create structure e.g. *screen is divided*
- often features a presenter / narrator who 'leads' the audience through the experience
- may include interviews with experts or member of the public e.g. *'a real madness in his eyes'*

b) Language

- language related to the topic
- informal language if interviews are used e.g. *what a beautiful deal*
- use of facts and statistics e.g. *on the tightrope for 45 minutes*
- may use voiceover
- may use persuasive language e.g. *It was wonderful*
- may use subtitles

c) Grammar

- spoken language, may be formal or informal
- sentence fragments
- may be past or present tense

This article about *Man on Wire** analyses and comments on some features of the documentary genre.

Not many documentaries have gained the notoriety that *Man on Wire* has achieved. This is due to the legendary and gripping story of Frenchman Philippe Petit's audacious walk on a tightrope between the Twin Towers in New York on 7 August 1974. The director, James Marsh, has ticked all the boxes for a fascinating insight into how this bold, history-making prank was achieved in his award-winning 2008 documentary film.

article's introduction provides background information / director named

The 134-minute documentary gives the viewer more than just a brief sky walk (and back) between two famous buildings. It provides background into Petit's passion for tightrope walking, showing him practising at an early age with his girlfriend. The actual sky walk on the famous day is detailed from the moment Petit and his team entered the South Tower disguised as workmen on the previous day. This is an elaborate procedure, made difficult by being a secret, illegal mission.

structure of documentary

a mixture of fact and opinion / use of statistics / background information

Also, the viewer is given an insight into the mind of Petit as he provides some of his own commentary in the documentary. 'If I die: what a beautiful deal — to die in the exercise of your passion.' This is his attitude to his dangerous lifestyle. There are also interviews and voiceover comments featuring his team and some of his friends.

persuasive language used by subject of documentary

detail / use of adjectives

One comment describes him as having 'a real madness in his eyes'. Other people defend his walk between the two towers with comments like it was 'against the law, but not wicked or mean. It was wonderful.' However, the clandestine nature of Petit's quest creates an atmosphere of excitement and suspense, even though the viewer knows the outcome.

quotations show comment and observations offered in the documentary

Another technique that keeps the viewer interested is the camerawork. At times, the screen is divided to tell two stories. The left-hand side shows the ongoing story of the walk across the two towers, while the right-hand side shows Petit as a child, sometimes using a child actor to re-enact these scenes. The screen alternates between black and white and colour photography. The most spectacular shots are those that show Petit as a tiny man on a thin rope, surrounded by sky, walking, kneeling, lying and bouncing on the tightrope for 45 minutes. At the end of the stunt he was arrested by police.

structure of the documentary

other techniques / opinionative language / terms related to the genre / descriptive language

Man on Wire is based on Philippe Petit's autobiography, *To Reach the Clouds*. It won awards at the 2008 Sundance Film Festival and in 2009 won a BAFTA for an 'Outstanding British Film', and an Academy Award for 'Best Documentary'.

article's background information / general conclusion

* Find the documentary itself and watch it!

1. Definition:

An **editorial** is the expression of the viewpoint of the newspaper on an issue, written by the editor or an experienced senior journalist.

2. Purpose and Role of Writer:

opinionative writing designed to persuade the reader to a point of view and sometimes to take action on a selected issue

3. Generic Features:

a) Structure and Organisation

- introduction: presents hypothesis or point of view e.g. *the cenotaph be moved ...*
- some background information on the issue may be given e.g. *Christchurch sculptor*
- each paragraph:
  - — supports the basic argument presented in the introduction
  - — has a clear topic sentence and then elaborates on the issue giving one reason or example per paragraph; a logical and sequential development
- opinion is supported with factual evidence
- conclusion: sometimes a strong statement, or a call for action to readers e.g. *To move it would be unthinkable*
- no byline as it is the newspaper's opinion, not the Editor's

b) Language

- headline: short and sometimes clever; using humour or irony and an authoritative tone e.g. *must stay*
- language: persuasive, sometimes emotive language used to hook readers e.g. *entirely inappropriate; strikingly beautiful*
- formal educated language
- statistics used to support the arguments e.g. *73 years*
- use of linking words e.g. *In the meantime*

c) Grammar

- complex sentences mixed with shorter ones for emphasis
- longer paragraphs than in a news article
- rhetorical questions may be posed
- third person point of view though sometimes the inclusive 'we'/ 'our' or the adversarial 'they' / 'them' is used e.g. *it occupies a unique place*
- present tense e.g. *It is cut off now*

Cenotaph must stay in the Square

headline's verb offers authority

alliteration

OPINION:

introduces issue

The suggestion that the cenotaph be moved from its site next to Christ Church Cathedral is understandable. Since the earthquake of February 2011, the memorial, the traditional location for commemorations of Anzac Day for *73 years*, has been inaccessible. For months, while the red-zone cordon was in place, it could not even be seen. Since the cordon was lifted, it has been visible but has remained fenced off. It is likely to stay that way for as long as it takes to get the cathedral repaired or rebuilt.

uses statistics

In the meantime, Anzac Day ceremonies have been held far from the memorial in Cranmer Square. There is also the possibility that any new cathedral may make moving it a necessity, which is why thoughts of a permanent move to Cranmer Square have arisen. Moving it from Cathedral Square would, though, be entirely inappropriate. It would also be a peculiar twist in its history, considering it took some time to get it on to the site in the first place.

states paper's opinion

ellipsis marks (…) show part of article has been omitted

...

Christchurch sculptor William Trethewey and architect George Hart designed the memorial, starting, it is said, from a pencil sketch made by Trethewey during a lunchtime. Gould's idea was that the memorial should be "an emblem of peace rather . . . than war" and the five allegorical figures around it are to Youth, Sacrifice, Justice, Valour and Peace. The central figure holding a sword being broken had been intended to be called Victory but the memorial committee rejected that and it has no name. The memorial was unveiled in 1937.

background provided; anecdote; quotation

passive voice

For all the travails involved in its creation, it occupies a unique place in the life of Christchurch. To move it would be unthinkable. It is a strikingly beautiful and dignified work of art that honours all those who have died in defence of the country. It has come to be the heart of the city's Anzac Day ceremonies. Its central location underlines its solemn central significance. It is cut off now, but that is temporary. The fences will eventually come down and it will again be possible to lay wreaths on it in the centre of the city, where it should be.

formal language; complex sentences; strong vocabulary

strong vocabulary

restates opinion firmly

The Press

1. Definition:

A **comparative essay** compares two similar or contrasting subjects. A **general comparative essay** may compare places, people or ideas. A **comparative literary essay** will compare two texts.

2. Purpose:

to inform, and in some cases persuade the reader about the similarities and differences between two things

3. Generic Features:

a) Structure and Organisation

- a comparative essay should have a logical structure
- introduction should
  - — make at least one general comment that links the two items e.g. *both describe*
  - — present a clear point of view, even if it's neutral e.g. *individual facing a personal challenge by personal choice*
- body should
  - — devote equal space to both texts / subjects, one at a time or interlinked
  - — may outline the comparison between the two in a separate paragraph
  - — provide sufficient general background information e.g. *relives the accident; spent four years alone*
  - — conclusion will summarise the essay's general points e.g. *Both the texts reveal how personal experience helps…*
- each paragraph should begin with a topic sentence for clarity e.g. *The writer shows the surfer building the waves in his mind*
- examples, quotations, statistics to strengthen the argument e.g. *'feelings of helplessness'; 'dejected, languid, and melancholy'*

b) Language

- formal, informative, generally persuasive
- comparative words e.g. *Similarly; In contrast*
- linking words e.g. *Both; However; whether*

c) Grammar

- correct sentence structure
- appropriate paragraphing
- present tense
- third person e.g. *he; it; they*

Facing a personal challenge can affect an individual's confidence and belief in themselves. Discuss with reference to a fictional and nonfiction text.

The Last of the Invisible Sharks, a fictional short story by John O'Brien, and Richard Steele's essay *Alexander Selkirk* both describe an individual facing a personal challenge by personal choice.

introduction restates question and makes a comparative comment

The unnamed surfer in the short story has experienced an accident surfing at a beach, to which he and his friends have returned to surf. He sits 'quiet and uneasy' in the car with his excited friends. On arriving at the beach he is reluctant to enter the water, doing campsite chores instead, but eventually decides to go in and avoid the larger waves. The writer shows the surfer's increasing confidence with a smaller wave but 'uncertainty seized him' and his fear causes him to be twisted and dragged beneath a larger wave. He decides to get ashore and 'never ride the dangerous break again' as he relives the accident, which he thought at the time would kill him but actually meant just plaster and stitches.

background information

The writer shows the surfer building the waves in his mind, frightening himself. 'They were silent, terror-filled mountains, cold and dark, ready to fill the surfer's universe with a turbulent horror.' To reach the shore he needs 'to shake off his feelings of helplessness and think clearly.'

topic sentence

quotation

He notices his friends signalling from the shore and believes they are telling him there is a shark in the water. He is now a 'confused mass of fear' but has to decide what to do. Which is worse? Eaten by a shark or smashed by a monstrous wave? He chooses the wave, and surfs to safety. 'He felt he had completed a near impossible task', surfing an eight-metre wave (which turns out to really be just five!). His friends had actually wanted to know where he had put the beer, so the story ends on a light-hearted note as the writer implies that the surfer had conquered his fear and put his world back into balance.

concludes comment on first text

Similarly, Alexander Selkirk (on whose adventure Robinson Crusoe is thought to have been based) faces a personal challenge. He requested to be left on an island, Juan Fernandez, near Chile, as he thought the ship he was on was not seaworthy and with whose captain he has 'irreconcilable differences'. He spent four years alone before being rescued and one account of his story is told in an essay by Richard Steele published in a magazine in 1712.

topic sentence, using comparative word

Selkirk has to survive by finding food, shelter, water and eventually clothing for himself. At first he is frightened by huge sea lions and has just goats, cats and rats for company. He had basic equipment, such as a knife, hatchet and kettle, and the useful experience of being a sailor to help him survive physically. However, his biggest challenge was loneliness. Steele points out that a sailor spends most of his time in the company of others, and describes how Selkirk was kept busy getting food and water and building shelter, but when this was organised he 'grew dejected, languid, and melancholy, scarce able to refrain from doing himself Violence'.

interesting details

writer's insight

Steele tells how by 'Force of Reason' and reading the scriptures, Selkirk came to accept his position and eventually enjoy his time alone on the island; he is described as 'strong and cheerful', a man who has developed great self-confidence from survival.

concludes comment on second text

In contrast to the short story writer, Steele tells the reader what to think, spelling out the 'moral' of the tale 'that he is happiest who confines his Wants to natural Necessities'.

points out a contrast between texts

Both the texts reveal how personal experience helps a person to face a challenge successfully when it is necessary for survival, whether real, as in Selkirk's case, or imaginary, as in the case of the unnamed surfer.

conclusion refers to key words of question

1. Definition:

A **persuasive essay** presents a writer's point of view on an issue.

2. Purpose and Role of Writer:

to inform (expository); to inform and persuade on an issue (argumentative / persuasive)

3. Generic Features:

a) Structure and Organisation

- exposition / argument structure: informing / outlining point of view and substantiating it
- general introduction e.g. Foodism ... *food images*
- body: developing the argument
- conclusion e.g. *Food, with a capital 'F', has become a four-letter word.*
- logical development
- topic sentences to open each paragraph
- each paragraph needs explanation and evidence to develop the argument
- final sentence of each paragraph is a clincher e.g. *Obesity is the scourge of the West ...*

b) Language

- formal language e.g. *Daily, we're bombarded with food images*
- specialised language relating to the issue e.g. food: *gluttony; cholesterol; harvest*
- persuasive language e.g. adjectives: *glossy; mouth-watering*

c) Grammar

- paragraph format linked with appropriate vocabulary e.g. *Although ...*
- complex sentences
- present tense e.g. *Foodism is becoming a lifestyle*
- impersonal, but 'you' and 'we' are used as inclusive pronouns

Persuasive Essay

Foodism has become a popular fad in the New Zealand in recent years. Daily, we're bombarded with food images: from cooking shows on television to glossy mouth-watering magazines for sale in newsagents and supermarkets.

·········· topic sentence

·········· adjectives

Foodism is becoming a lifestyle. Not only is dining out regarded as a leisure activity in itself these days, but fast food restaurants serving fat-laden, carbohydrate-loaded products to the younger generation are accepted as the norm. You may find the odd healthy green leaf inside your burger or wrap, but this is just a token gesture to appease nutritionists and other health professionals.

·········· complex sentence

·········· addresses audience

For a free health check, visit the annual Healthy Living Expo held at the Dunedin Convention and Exhibition Centre during July. It's a chance for everyone who is overweight, obese or over-indulgent to have their blood pressure and cholesterol checked on the spot. This could curtail food orgies of the future.

·········· informative content

At a time when the US is forcing free lap bands around ever-expanding middle America, New Zealanders are becoming foodaholics with growing fervour. We have forgotten that like our American cousins, we are among the fattest nations on earth. And getting fatter.

·········· inclusive pronouns

It is a well-known cliché that the West spends more on diets than the East spends on food. Initially, we spend to indulge our gastronomic gluttony, then we spend millions absorbing the ideas of Atkins, Montignac and other diet gurus, some of them deceased. Obesity is the scourge of the West, as AIDS is the enemy in developing countries.

·········· persuasive language

·········· alliteration

Although historically associated with sensuous pleasure and the celebration of the harvest, food has now been elevated beyond its original function. Food, with a capital 'F', has become a four-letter word. And that's obscene.

·········· strong ending

·········· alliteration and humour

1. Definition:

A **feature article** is an article written to give more depth to the news. Written by an expert, it gives background information on a newsworthy topic as well as the writer's personal slant or experience.

2. Purpose and Role of Writer:

to inform and entertain, and sometimes to persuade

3. Generic Features:

a) Structure and Organisation

- headline should be attention grabbing e.g. *The most powerful woman in the world?*
- subheading e.g. *On track to head up ...*
- byline e.g. *Nicola Russell*
- column format
- introduction should hook readers and establish a point of view through direct statement, example or rhetorical question e.g. *Helen Clark remains right at home*
- narrative rather than inverted pyramid structure

b) Language

- creative and colourful e.g. *no-nonsense demeanour*
- use of anecdotes or background information e.g. *walking on the beach in Waihi*
- personal references may be used
- figurative language may be used e.g. *keep her distance*
- writer creates relationship with reader through an individual writing style
- expansive, not economical, in length

c) Grammar

- third person usual but use of first person is acceptable
- variety of long and short sentences
- present tense e.g. *She's our first elected female Prime Minister*

The most powerful woman in the world?

On track to head up the United Nations, Helen Clark has made a huge impact globally since she was our Prime Minister. She sits down with Nicola Russell to talk about juggling her public persona with her private life.

She's our first elected female Prime Minister, and in the running for one of the world's most powerful positions, but Helen Clark remains right at home on the streets of New Zealand.

As she crosses a busy Auckland road, heads turn and she is stopped for a picture. She's friendly and relaxed but with the self-contained, no-nonsense demeanour of someone who commands respect.

With more than five years heading up the United Nations Development Programme (UNDP) under her belt, Helen is arguably the most globally influential person to come out of New Zealand. But on her biannual trips home she steps back into the role of dedicated daughter, walking on the beach in Waihi with her elderly father, George Clark, and filling his freezer with his favourite meals.

'He likes my chilli con carne, beef and beer stew, pork and pineapple, and mild lamb curry,' she says, listing his requests with a chuckle. 'I make him a selection — I try to leave forty to sixty meals in the freezer.'

On her latest visit, family has been even more of a priority than usual. Determined to keep her distance from political affairs, Helen has turned down most speaking invitations. She's arrived smack bang on election time and admits she doesn't miss New Zealand politics.

'I have moved on,' she says with a decisive nod. 'I think you have to leave it to the next generation of people — I see the news and that's about it.'

…

Deeply engaged in her current role, she says she doesn't have a long-term plan, and if she doesn't become the Secretary-General she knows 'life will never be empty'. What she is sure about is New Zealand is the place she will call home again. 'I'll definitely retire here.'

Annotations (margin notes):

- rhetorical question as headline; catches attention; largest font
- subheading provides angle of article, and byline; uses mid-size, different font
- intro paragraph links position and person
- supports the dual nature of the subject
- informative content
- human interest anecdote, as story is for a women's magazine
- topical detail
- vocabulary supports point of view
- ellipsis marks (…) show part of article has been omitted
- conclusion, links back to angle of article

---

1. Definition:

A **film review** is an analysis or appreciation of the quality of a film.

2. Purpose and Role of Writer:

to inform and persuade / criticise

3. Generic Features:

a) Structure and Organisation

- introduction
  — should include title and director and main actors
  — needs an angle / general opinionative comment
    e.g. *will become a classic New Zealand film*
- brief plot analysis e.g. *Genesis Potini, bipolar, poor*
- ending not revealed e.g. *how he tries to help*
- analysis of key aspects of the film in a paragraph for each
  — key narrative techniques include: theme, plot, genre, characters, setting
  — key film features include: camerawork, acting, dialogue
  — include opinions on the quality of these aspects
    e.g. *completely convincing*
- may use key quotes from the dialogue
- provides some background on the director and the origin of the film
- may make comparisons with other films by the director or in the same genre
- written in column format, according to the word limit

b) Language

- formal
- literary and film language e.g. *dialogue; flashbacks*
- informative and opinionative e.g. *selected for the 2014 Toronto International Film Festival*
- impersonal language is the safe option, but reviewer may address reader

c) Grammar

- correct English is expected most of the time
- sentence fragments may be used for emphasis
- first person is optional, but should be limited to one or two comments
- present tense creates immediacy

Film Review:
THE DARK HORSE

strong opinionative comments supported by facts ....

THE DARK HORSE, directed by Wellington-born James Napier Robertson, will become a classic New Zealand film. Based on a 2002 documentary by Jim Marbrook, it is a splendid film that has been selected for the 2014 Toronto International Film Festival.

outlines plot briefly ....

Genesis Potini, bipolar, poor, with a troubled family is nevertheless a speed-chess champion. He becomes involved in teaching the local children to play, believing it will help them control their lives. He wants to help his nephew, Mana, whose father wants him to become a gang member, too.

comments on quality of acting ....

Cliff Curtis and James Rolleston are completely convincing as the difficult Genesis and the troubled Mana.

and film techniques ....

Clever camerawork reveals Genesis's delusions and potential to sink back into madness and the dialogue between the main characters is finely scripted to be completely believable.

The film is set in small-town New Zealand and over a short period of time but uses flashbacks to show something about Genesis's childhood. The poverty and narrowness of this world is shown especially as it contrasts with the big city world of the competition the children enter.

.... *setting and techniques commented on*

The film is about a man who finds a refuge in chess and how he tries to help others use chess to help themselves. It is a sympathetic exploration of hope to escape poverty of the mind and the cruel world of gangs. It is a superb New Zealand film that should be seen and enjoyed by all New Zealanders.

.... *conclusion makes overall assessment of purpose and success*

1. Definition:

A **letter of application** for a job is a letter that responds to a specific position.

2. Purpose and Role of Writer:

to gain employment by impressing a prospective employer with relevant content and competent writing skills

3. Generic Features:

a) Structure and Organisation

- sender's address is set out at the top on the left side of the page
- the date is placed underneath
- receiver's title and name, company name and address are set out below the date
- standard greeting e.g. *Dear*
- the body of the letter is structured logically: introductory, explanatory and concluding paragraphs
- some use of persuasive language e.g. *topped my year; good social skills*

b) Language

- formal (not impersonal) language e.g. *as advertised in* The Local News
- terminology specific to business letters e.g. *Yours faithfully*
- concise and clear
- positive, enthusiastic tone

c) Grammar

- formal grammar
- present tense e.g. *I am also an outgoing person*
- first person e.g. *I am writing*

1 King Street
Masterton 5885 ·········|···· correct layout / format

1 February 2015

The Editor
The Local News
1 Main Street
Masterton 5810

Dear Sir/Madam

I am writing to apply for the position of cadet reporter as ···········|··· clear statement of purpose
advertised in *The Local News* on Saturday, 30 November.

I have just completed Year 13 at Masterton High School, where ········|·· background factual information
I topped my year in English, and was editor of the school
newsletter. Next year I hope to enrol in a part-time degree in
Journalism at Victoria University.

Not only do I love writing, but my teachers and the school's ········|·· personal qualities appropriate for the position
Careers Counsellor have advised me to pursue my talents in
this area. I am also an outgoing person with good social skills
and the ability to work in a team.

For two years I have worked as a waitress at Café Bellissima in ········|·· previous experience
Coffeetown. Here I have learnt communication skills and how
to interact with the public. I know this experience will stand me ········|·· skills acquired
in good stead in the newspaper industry. ········|··· link to new position

I look forward to hearing from you.

Yours faithfully ·········|··· standard closure

Ann Applicant

Ann Applicant

1. Definition:

A **résumé** is a record of personal details that is attached to the letter. A résumé contains a written summary of educational qualifications, employment history and personal details. It is also called a curriculum vitae (CV).

2. Purpose and Role of Writer:

to gain employment

3. Generic Features:

a) Structure and Organisation

- arranged chronologically according to the definition above
- list structure with headings
- summary list format
- logical sequence
- attractively formatted
- designed for ease and speed of reading

b) Language

- concise but formal
- factual and accurate

c) Grammar

- sentence format
- sentence fragments
- third person
- past tense to describe past achievements

Résumé

Name: Ann Applicant

Address: 1 King Street

                   Masterton 5885

Telephone: (06) 384 444

Email: annapplicant@hotmail.com

.... correct layout and format

.... logically structured response

Education: Masterton Primary School (2002–2009)

                   Masterton High School (2010–2014)

                   NCEA L3 completed — 2014

.... use of dates for clarity

Employment: Cafe Bellissima: Coffeetown (2013–2014)

                   Duties include: table service, barista, some food preparation.

.... clear description of tasks and skills

                   Pizza Palace: King Street, Masterton (2012)

                   Duties included: taking orders across the counter and by telephone, some food preparation, use of cash register.

                   The City News: 1 Elizabeth Street, City (2012–2013)

                   Duties included: folding and adding inserts to newspapers, delivery of newspapers.

Personal Qualifications:

                   Dux of English 2012, 2014

                   Debating Captain 2014

                   Editor of the school newsletter 2012, 2014

                   Student editor of the school annual 2014

                   Girl Guide Leader 2012, 2013

                   Member of Second IV Tennis 2012

.... evidence of applicant's qualities

Referees: Maria Bellissima, Cafe Proprietor —

                   Ph: (06) 3010 0000

                   Susan English, Teacher, Masterton High

                   School — Ph: (06) 370 5611

.... contact details of referees

1. Definition:

A **job interview** is a meeting between an employer and a prospective employee.

2. Purpose and Role of Writer:

the employer's purpose is to choose the most suitable applicant for the job through effective questioning. The prospective employee's role is to persuade the employer or interviewer that he or she is the most suitable person for the job

3. Generic Features:

a) Structure and Organisation

- interviewer will determine the structure of the interview e.g. *So you want to be a journalist?*

- he or she will provide some background information about the job and expectations e.g. *Well, let me tell you*

- interviewer is likely to refer to the applicant's written application / résumé to develop a line of questioning e.g. *And I see you're good at English*

- interviewer will probably cover the three aspects in the résumé: education, previous employment and personal qualifications, by questioning the prospective employee in more detail e.g. *And do you think your results will be good enough to get you into journalism at university?*

- interviewee must make eye contact with the employer and respond clearly and concisely, with honesty, sincerity and interest. Be positive.

- at the end of or during the interview, the interviewee will be encouraged to ask questions about the job. These should be carefully thought out, and not merely concerned with pay and conditions e.g. *How long do you think it will be before I publish a story?*

b) Language

- informal but deferential (showing respect)

- politeness, combined with an enthusiastic tone of voice essential

- good vocabulary, especially related to the terminology of the job e.g. *word processing; editing the school newsletter*

c) Grammar

- correct grammar

- spoken mode so sentence fragments are acceptable

- first person

Mr Employer:	Good morning, Ann. (indicating a seat)
Ann Applicant:	Good morning, Mr Employer. (sits)
Mr Employer:	So you want to be a journalist?
Ann Applicant:	(looking at him) Yes. I decided on my chosen career two years ago, after I began editing the school newsletter.
Mr Employer:	And I see you're good at English.
Ann Applicant:	Yes, it's my favourite subject.
Mr Employer:	And do you think your results will be good enough to get you into journalism at university?
Ann Applicant:	I think so. I certainly hope so.
Mr Employer:	And what about your word processing skills? And computer literacy?
Ann Applicant:	I learnt word processing at school. I'm quite fast and accurate.
Mr Employer:	Good. Well, let me tell you a little about the job. We'll train you by sending you out with one of our senior journalists. She'll show you how to gather information and interview people. Then she'll show you how to write a story. We'll begin with small stories. You'll be required to do some office work and general errands too. How does that sound?
Ann Applicant:	Great. How long do you think it will be before I publish a story?
Mr Employer:	Well, that really depends on you and your expertise. Of course it's only a part-time position. We'll give you time off to attend your lectures.
Ann Applicant:	Thank you. And is there any likelihood that this position will become a full-time one when I graduate?
Mr Employer:	Yes, there's every possibility that we'll keep you on after graduation if you prove satisfactory.
Ann Applicant:	That's great.
Mr Employer:	Now your CV looks very good, Ann. We just have one or two more applicants to interview before we make a final decision. We'll let you know by Friday. Now do you have any other questions?
Ann Applicant:	Just one. How can I prepare myself for the job? I read a lot of newspapers on the internet and keep up with current affairs.
Mr Employer:	That's a great start. Keep reading and learning. And we'll let you know by the end of the week …

Annotations:
- relevant, definite answers / concise responses
- honest, sincere response
- positive attitude / enthusiasm
- questions show enthusiasm and competence
- question shows interest and confidence

1. Definition:

A **business letter** is a procedural form of communication. Any letter that is not personal (i.e. to family or friends) is considered a business letter.

2. Purpose and Role of Writer:

to seek or impart information of a personal business or general business nature

3. Generic Features:

a) Structure and Organisation

- sender's address set out on the left side of the page
- the date placed below the sender's address
- receiver's title and name, company name and address set out below the date
  e.g. *The Manager, Toptech Ltd*
- the standard greeting: e.g. *Dear*; the closure: e.g. *Yours faithfully*
- logical structure in the body of the letter: introductory, explanatory and concluding paragraphs

b) Language

- impersonal language e.g. *for no apparent reason; If repairs can be completed*
- business terminology e.g. *entitled; acceptable quality; matter settled*
- concise and direct e.g. *I have attached a copy of the sales docket*
- tone is polite and businesslike

c) Grammar

- formal grammar
- complex sentences
- first person e.g. *I consider seven days*
- present tense e.g. *I am prepared to accept*

1 Wellington Road
Wellington 6013

1 March 2015

The Manager
Toptech Ltd
1 Company Road
Porirua 5024

Dear Sir/Madam

I am writing to complain about the Hearwell Headphones, model 14HW, which I bought at your Wellington shop on 25 January 2015.

They worked reasonably well for about one month and then for no apparent reason only one earpiece produced sound. A week later neither earpiece worked. I am very disappointed with this piece of equipment.

I understand I am entitled to expect the things I buy are of acceptable quality. I am sure you will agree that in view of the above problems the headphones were not of a reasonable standard.

I am prepared to accept a repair of the headphones at no cost to me. If repairs can be completed quickly and effectively, I will consider the matter settled.

I attach a copy of the sales docket as proof of purchase.

Please telephone me to arrange for the repair to be carried out. I consider seven days to be a fair time to have the headphones back in full working order.

Yours faithfully

John Payne

John Payne

standard layout and format

clear statement of purpose / clear statement or the problem

concise outline of the problem presents a strong case and a legitimate complaint

conclusion suggests a polite but firm request for action

1. Definition:

A **letter to the editor** is a formal letter written to a newspaper. Most letters are now sent by email.

2. Purpose and Role of Writer:

to express an opinion on an issue

3. Generic Features:

a) Structure and Organisation

- use business letter format if sending by mail
- if emailing use the greeting *Sir/Madam* or Dear Sir/Madam
- introduction outlines the topic and the writer's opinion e.g. *We live in a society*
- body paragraphs develop the argument logically, point by point, including rebuttal
- topic sentences provide clear signposts e.g. *the media is clearly to blame*
- conclusion restates opinion, or is a call to action or solution e.g. *They deserve better!*

b) Language

- formal / impersonal e.g. *The cult of celebrity is used*
- vocabulary appropriate to the issue raised
- informative but also forceful and persuasive e.g. *Isn't it a shame*
- use of examples e.g. *Miley Cyrus, Lady Gaga and Nicki Minaj*
- use of statistics e.g. *barely in double figures*
- dramatic, emotional, or use of irony to provoke a response from readers e.g. *little more than a few feathers and fishnets*
- topic sentences as signposts e.g. *No wonder the young girls of today*

c) Grammar

- complete and correct sentences and paragraphs
- present or past tense e.g. *No wonder the family is in decline*
- first person is acceptable, as is second and third person. Second person (you) or first person plural (we) may be used as a form of persuasion e.g. *I believe*
- rhetorical questions are effective e.g. *What sort of future is this for the young of today?*

standard greeting

Sir/Madam

clear opening, presenting clear point of view with examples

We live in a society that has lost its way. **And** I believe that the media is largely to blame. Newspapers, like your own, and magazines, are fixated on wealth and beauty. The cult of celebrity is used to sell magazines and to suck the unsuspecting public into living vicariously through their pop or sporting idols.

use of rhetorical questions / topic sentences to signpost argument / examples

What sort of values are being passed down to the next generation by celebrities who have left their wives for other celebrity trophy partners? Isn't it a shame that such talent is so misdirected? And it's not only sportsmen who are guilty of behaving badly and presenting as poor role models to the younger generation. Pop stars like Miley Cyrus, Lady Gaga and Nicki Minaj appear on stage these days wearing little more than a few feathers and fishnets.

sentence fragments for impact / emotive language

No wonder the young girls of today are so inappropriately underdressed. Not only teenagers either. Young girls aged barely in double figures are aspiring Mileys and Barbies. Even office wear has undergone a revolution, with cleavage being a seemingly acceptable fashion for office and professional staff alike.

The media is clearly to blame for this outrage and the print media especially. Women's magazines have reached an all-time low in taste and modesty. Actresses, married one day and divorced the next, or not married at all, are treated like royalty. Even the standards of the royal family have slipped over the last few years. No wonder the family is in decline as a stable institution. What sort of future is this for the young of today? They deserve better!

dramatic conclusion and final sentence

A. Wowser

Marylands

Today there is an abundance of choice for teens, even in the genre of teenage romance. The shelves of school and local libraries are packed with intriguing titles, often with pink-coloured covers. The audience for these, as with their adult equivalent, is generally female.

1. Definition:

Young adult fiction describes texts that are written and published for a teenage market.

2. Purpose and Role of Writer:

to interest teenagers in reading and purchasing a product

3. Generic Features:

a) Structure and Organisation

- narrative / story structure
- chapter format — often fast-moving, short chapters
- plot — usually dramatic and suspenseful, involving conflict between teenagers or with adults
- characters — main protagonist is generally a teenage character
- setting — usually familiar — home, school, etc.
- narrative voice — action is seen through the eyes of a teenage hero or heroine

b) Language

- must be suitable to a teenage audience
- should replicate contemporary teen expressions, lifestyle and icons
- dialogue must be realistic according to character and situation
- description should be brief and visual so as not to interrupt the story line
- style may be reflective if first person is used
- depending on audience age, swearing and some sexually explicit material is acceptable
- writing style must create atmosphere and strong emotion to maintain audience interest

c) Grammar

- written in first or third person
- may use multiple narration
- mixture of simple and complex sentences
- dialogue use may be ungrammatical, depending on characters' ages and level of education
- adjectives and adverbs are used in moderation
- present or past tense may be used

Here is an extract from *Iron Butterfly*, a romantic narrative by Claire Edward.

The Choice: Jessica Gray is torn between her feelings for her old boyfriend, 'bad boy' surfer Matt, who has already two-timed her with 'bikini girl', and her new boyfriend, Peter, who is reliable and devoted to her. Which one should she choose?

····· content is suitable for older teens

'I'll pick you up at eight,' Peter whispered in Jess's ear. He squeezed her arm gently and walked off towards his car ...

····· opens with dialogue

The Surf Club was transformed into a nightclub with swirling lights. It was packed with local surfers. Most of the guys were looking uncomfortable in black tie outfits, like they'd rather be in board shorts, barefoot, with their feet in the water. Jess's heart jumped when she spotted Matt leaning against the wall, alone, in the far corner of the room, devastatingly handsome in his dinner suit. He was staring at her. Was it in admiration? Jess knew she stood out in her low-cut, scarlet dress. Especially when Peter led her onto the dance floor.

brief description creates visual effect / past tense / setting appeals to teen audience

It was impossible to speak over the music, so Jess didn't notice the punch coming. One minute, Peter was standing close to her, the next he was in a crumpled heap on the floor. He'd melted to the floor like a warm ice-cream, before she could reach her hand out to stop him, and before she could turn around to see what had happened.

third person narrative seen through the eyes of the main protagonist, Jess

But there was no need for Jess to turn. Who else would the punch come from? Not only was Matt suddenly beside her, but he was obviously drunk. He swayed in front of her like one of the streamers that were beginning to detach themselves from the walls. Matt, too, was unattached. He looked so alone. No bikini girl. No mates. He opened his mouth, but no words came out. Instead he lurched towards her and vomited on her left shoe.

use of question form to signify reflection of main character

Lucky they'd hired security for the night. A burly man in a dark uniform rushed over and escorted Matt to the door. The music stopped and everyone on the dance floor was staring from Jess to Matt to Pete, and whispering.

strong dramatic action features in this incident

Pete grinned weakly at her as he rose from the floor. Someone in the crowd passed her a handful of paper napkins. She removed her silver shoe and wiped it carefully, trying not to breathe in the mingled smell of alcohol and vomit.

attention to detail / contrasting personalities of male characters shown

'C'mon,' she whispered to Pete. 'Let's get out of here.' The last thing she saw was the security guard pushing Matt into a taxi. Matt's reflection in the back window showed that he had sobered up enough to realise that he'd 'stuffed up'. He gave Jess a sad little smile. She turned away quickly. Could she bring herself to forgive him again?

uncertain chapter ending creates suspense

1. Definition:

A **novel** is fictional prose of considerable length, which uses the actions, speech and thoughts of the characters to tell a story.

2. Purpose and Role of Writer:

to entertain the reader with a story; to bring an idea or theme to life; to earn a living by writing a novel people will buy

3. Generic Features:

a) Structure and Organisation

- a plot involving the major character / s: usually orientation / introduction, complication / problem, resolution / conclusion
- possibly sub or secondary plots about minor characters
- a setting: time, place and social background
- divided into chapters; may be chronological or use flashbacks
- narrative voice, one or more than one

b) Language

- appropriate to audience
- dialogue to reveal characters
- description to advance plot and show setting
- vocabulary appropriate to content
- descriptive writing will include adjectives, adverbs, effective verbs, etc.

c) Grammar

- may use first person narrator (I) or third person narrative voice (he, she, they)
- accurate use of English in complete sentences, unless dialogue or narrative voice demands incorrect English
- variety of sentence structure depending on content
- past tense is more common, but present or future tense may be used (in fact any tense!)

Novels can be found in books, on Kindles, serialised in magazines, on the internet.

From: **The 10pm Question** by Kate De Goldi

Tuesday the fourteenth of February began badly for Frankie Parsons. There was no milk for his Just Right. There was no Go-Cat for The Fat Controller, so The Fat Controller stood under the table meowing accusingly while Frankie ate his toast.

establishes character, time of year, time of day, modern domestic setting; third person narrative voice; past tense.

The newspaper hadn't arrived, which meant Frankie couldn't take a headline and article for Current Affairs, and so would earn one of Mr. A's sardonic looks; nor could he check the weather report for humidity. Humidity levels were important to Frankie, and for two reasons: one, a cricket ball swung rather trickily and lethally when the air was heavy, which was a good thing. Two, ants appeared in droves when the temperature was warm and the atmosphere thick, which was a very bad thing. Frankie nursed a special hatred for ants.

offers more details about main character — age, personality, leisure interest, a particular dislike

So, Tuesday the fourteenth began badly, and continued that way. Frankie's sister, Gordana, had swiped the last muesli bar and the only crisp apple; there was no bus money in his mother's wallet so Frankie had to search for a nail file in order to prise out ten-cent pieces from the emergency pink china pig.

another character introduced; age - appropriate vocabulary; family setting fleshed out a little

…

'This house doesn't work!' Frankie called up the stairs. He stuffed his exercise books, lunch bag and sneakers into his backpack. Then he stood very still and mentally perused the school day. This was his habit each morning. It was so he wouldn't forget anything. He was really very organised.

dialogue begins; action described

writer comments on main character

…

'A bad workman always blames his tools,' said Gordana. She came thumping down the stairs in her flat-footed, truculent, morning way. Gordana maintained she wasn't a morning person. In Frankie's private view his sister was a no-time person, not morning, afternoon, nor evening. The less he saw of her the better.

use of dialogue and action to reveal character

narrator reveals Frankie's thoughts and feelings — he is the main character

'Whadda you mean, a bad workman?' he said, and instantly regretted it. He really didn't know why he ever responded to Gordana. It always ended badly. Every day he told himself to ignore her and every day he ignored himself instead.

spelling reveals colloquial speech

Face it, Gigs had told him. You hate her. It's official. And mutual. Your sister is your enemy. Stop consorting.

another character introduced; short sentences used for effect — summarising Gigs' opinions.

1. Definition:

A **news article** is an account of the important news of the day.

2. Purpose and Role of Writer:

to provide accurate facts about a specific event

3. Generic Features:

a) Structure and Organisation

- headline: short, catchy or cleverly worded and summarises the angle of the article; use of alliteration or a play on words is a common device e.g. *season in Samoa*

- may use subheading: brief but gives more detail

- byline: the reporter's name

- inverted pyramid structure: important information first — major points to minor points; allows for readers to skim read and for editing quickly to meet a publishing deadline

- introduction: 5Ws and the 1H (i.e. who, what, where, when, why and how) as well as the angle / point of view of the article e.g. *All Blacks; World Cup; Samoan sun in July next year; defence; milestone agreement*

- body of the article: factual details and quotes from witnesses or experts; short paragraphs for easy reading, containing one main fact or idea e.g. *at Apia Park*

- conclusion: unimportant because the article may be shortened to fit into the newspaper at the last minute

- written in column format

- a lead / front page or important article may have a photograph of the event

b) Language

- simple vocabulary

- clear factual writing

- use of third person e.g. *It is well documented*

- concise and economical

c) Grammar

- short sentences

- short paragraphs

- third person / present tense / past tense / future tense

All Blacks to start 2015 test season in Samoa

By Daniel Richardson

The All Blacks' charge to their World Cup defence will begin in the Samoan sun in July next year.

A milestone agreement was confirmed this afternoon at New Zealand Rugby House in Wellington that will see the All Blacks meet Samoa in Apia for the first time on Wednesday, July 8.

The test match will kick-off at Apia Park at 3pm local time (2pm NZT) and will be the first Steven Hansen's men will play next season as they build towards next year's global tournament in England.

"It's the beginning of that 2015 season so it'll be a great way for us to start," Hansen said. "It'll be a great way to bring the guys together and it is going to be very special. We've got a lot of Samoan guys in the team who are proud of their heritage and we are very proud of them.

"You can only imagine what it's going to be like; 20,000 people can get in to the ground but there's going to be a lot more than that wanting to be part of it and we are looking forward to that.

"It's not just going there for a game, it's going there and learning a little bit about some of the heritage and more about the heritage of the people we have in our team and that's pretty special for us."

Samoan Prime Minister Tuilaepa Lupesoliai Sailele Malielegaoi, who is also chairman of the country's rugby union, said it would be an honour to host the All Blacks.

"It is well documented that New Zealand rugby has included many, many players of Pacific Island heritage, especially Samoans," he said.

"Our contributions to New Zealand rugby have been well known. It is therefore fitting that Manu Samoa will be hosting the All Blacks and I take this opportunity to express my very sincere appreciation for the support and work of so many people in making this rugby match possible."

...

Labour's Pacific Affairs spokesperson Su'a William Sio said the game was sure to "go down in history".

"Samoa, along with other Pacific nations, has given enormously to New Zealand, not least in the contributions from, among many, Frank Bunce, Michael Jones, Jerome Kaino, Keven Mealamu, Tana Umaga and Julian Savea to All Black rugby.

"I know there will be thousands travelling from New Zealand and around the Pacific to Samoa to watch this historic game. It will be rugby at its very best."

NZ Herald 9/9/14

Annotations:

- title clearly states topic
- byline
- introductory paragraphs state who, what, when, where, why, how
- column format
- background information/facts
- direct quotations from expert
- short paragraphs
- opinion of important people cited: indirectly and directly
- ellipsis marks (...) show lines omitted
- quoted opinion
- details to interest audience
- conclusion

1. Definition:

- A **nonfiction text** is a text that is factual or based on fact.

2. Purpose and Role of Writer:

- the purpose of nonfiction is to inform on a particular subject; the writer is generally some sort of expert in the field about which he or she is writing

- it may be in a book, a pamphlet or on the internet

3. Generic Features:

a) Structure and Organisation

- nonfiction usually
  — is divided into chapters or pages e.g. *Page 1— What is the bush?*
  — is in chronological in structure
  — is arranged according to subject matter
  — uses subheadings to organise content for easy reading
  — uses footnotes to identify sources

b) Language

- the language of nonfiction writing
  — may be formal or informal depending on the topic
  — may be specialist or generalist depending on the topic

c) Grammar

- the grammar used in nonfiction
  — depends on the topic of the text
  — may be written in first, second or third person, present or past tense
  — is usually conventional and correct, with complex sentences
  — uses specific terminology where appropriate

The New Zealand bush

Page 1 — What is the bush?

The bush: dense native forest

In New Zealand the primary meaning of 'bush' or 'native bush' is the indigenous forest.

Before humans arrived around 1250–1300 AD, 80% of the land was covered with trees. Early Maori cleared the forest in some areas, but when Pakeha arrived in the 19th century, some 50% of the country was still native forest.

The forest was evergreen and lush, and consisted of two main types: conifer-broadleaf dominating the North Island, and beech in much of the South Island. Under the tallest trees were layers of young trees, tree ferns and shrubs, and lower still were ferns and sedges. Vines and epiphytes thrived, and mosses and liverworts carpeted the ground. The result was a dense tangle — particularly before the introduction of browsing animals such as deer and possums in the 19th century.

The bush was very hard to travel through, and Europeans compared it to tropical vegetation. As early as 1841 people were using the term 'bush' as a synonym for jungle. This became the dominant meaning of the word in New Zealand. In 1896 the mountaineer A.P. Harper noted: 'In New Zealand the forest is always spoken of as "bush" as opposed to lower growth of vegetation, which is called "scrub".'[1]

Other meanings

The New Zealand usage of 'bush' probably comes from the word 'bosch', used by Dutch settlers in South Africa, where it meant uncultivated country. The word was then taken to Australia, where such areas were often parklike, with scattered eucalyptus and scrub (low-growing or stunted vegetation). So in Australia, 'the bush' is the outback, rather than dense forest.

On occasion the word was used in this sense in New Zealand too, meaning any area awaiting European settlement. *The Dictionary of New Zealand English* records a quotation from 1875: 'The Bush in colonial parlance means everywhere out of the towns, the bleak plains of Canterbury and the dreary uplands of Otago destitute of all vegetation save coarse tussock grass … are called the bush, as well as the impenetrable forests of lofty trees.'[2]

---

1   Arthur P. Harper, *Pioneer Work in the Alps of New Zealand*. London: T. Fisher Unwin, 1896, p. 32.
2   Quoted in H.W. Orsman, *The Dictionary of New Zealand English*. Auckland: Oxford University Press, 1999, p. 108.

Visit www.teara.govt.nz for the full article

Annotations (right margin):

factual title, divided into sections called pages on this website

subheading gives definition

introduction, definition extended/repeated

use of facts, data; complex and compound sentences

specific terminology; formal language; examples

educated vocabulary

footnotes tell where the information originated

subheadings divide text to aid skimming

research presented in easy-to-understand sentences

1. Definition:

A **novel** is a story, a work of fiction that is longer than 40,000 words.

2. Purpose and Role of Writer:

to entertain; to persuade the reader to accept an idea or philosophy; to recreate a historical era; or to seek fame and/or commercial success

3. Generic Features:

a) Structure and Organisation

- plot usually comprises: orientation, complication, resolution
- sub or secondary plots
- usually divided into chapters
- early chapters: rising action including some minor crises
- the climax: the moment when the main character usually reaches a turning point
- characters: main character / hero or heroine and other subsidiary characters
- setting: usually creates a definite place, time and social setting
- single narrator or multiple narrators possible

b) Language

- description of places, people, events e.g. *The mountain, the constant backdrop of our lives*
- dialogue between characters e.g. '*... watch where you're stepping!*'
- action through the author or narrator's eyes e.g. *I could not bear to think of it.*
- reflection by the author or central character/s e.g. *I am not made of volcanic stone*
- appropriate to the content
- vocabulary may be formal, colloquial, poetic, figurative, symbolic e.g. '*... we'll all be murdered in our beds.*'

c) Grammar

- method of narration may be first, second or third person e.g. *I wanted to shout*
- past or present tense e.g. *The sun shone hot*
- need not be correct grammar in dialogue

From *A Respectable Girl* by Fleur Beale

There were so many rumours. I grew to dread the words *people say*, and *have you heard?*

People say HMS Niger is coming to anchor off New Plymouth.

Have you heard? There are five hundred Taranakis marching up from the south.

Have you heard? We'll all starve because the farmers won't be able to harvest the wheat before the war begins.

What war? I wanted to shout. Nobody had declared war.

The sun shone hot. The sky spread above us, blue and brilliant. The mountain, the constant backdrop of our lives, appeared far away, coloured in its summer hue of pale blue. On my way to and from the shop, I raised my eyes to it. It had overlooked centuries of battles. This too will pass, it seemed to say.

'So it will,' I muttered, 'but I am not made of volcanic stone that will survive the centuries.' My thoughts turned again to escape. To England. But only if I could take Jamie and Arama with me. Useless.

'Hannah Carstairs, watch where you're stepping!' Maggie Barrow, one of Polly's friends, bent and picked up a bundle of clothes I'd trodden on.

I helped her gather the things she'd dropped. 'Can I help you carry them, Mrs Barrow?' Have you come into town?'

She straightened and clasped the clothes to her chest along with her child. 'My husband said I had to. Take the children, he said, or we'll all be murdered in our beds.' She burst into tears and I walked with her to the house where they were to stay. We had to walk around to the gateway left in the fortification ditch men were digging to defend the town.

Maggie gestured at it. 'I hope they'll finish it soon. We'll all feel a lot safer when it's done.'

'My brothers are helping to dig it,' I told her. I didn't tell her they helped too, to break the bottles to throw in the bottom of it for I could not bear to think of it. Maori invaders would come barefooted. Pakeha defenders wore boots.

---

set in 1860s Taranaki

first person narrative voice

based around real, historical events

setting described: time of year and place

shows narrator's words and thoughts too

direct speech

description of action

historical detail included

narrator's feelings revealed

1. Definition:

An **essay on a novel** demonstrates knowledge and insight into a literary text.

2. Purpose and Role of Writer:

an academic essay that informs the reader by developing and proving a hypothesis in response to a set question

3. Generic Features:

a) Structure and Organisation

- introduction: names and responds to the topic
- body: develops the hypothesis in a series of logically sequenced paragraphs e.g. *The novel shows how gradually*
- conclusion: restates the hypothesis and sums up the argument with a final evaluative comment e.g. *over the time during which this novel is set*
- paragraph structure follows a set formula
  — topic sentences are the opening sentences of each paragraph
     e.g. *Hannah learns unpleasant things*
  — the body of the paragraph is an explanation or elaboration of the general opening statement
  — each paragraph should then provide examples from the text being analysed, or a quotation from the text e.g. *'for a girl who could not believe in gooseberry bushes'*
  — the final sentence of the paragraph concludes this aspect of the argument and may provide a link to the next paragraph

b) Language

- formal language
- linking words e.g. *also; But when*
- conclusive words e.g. *over the time*

c) Grammar

- complex sentences
- paragraph structure
- quotations from the text e.g. *'a useful one'*
- third person e.g. *Hannah learns*
- present tense e.g. *At the beginning of the novel Hannah is young, only 15*

Analyse how a main character OR individual matures and takes action in a text (or texts) you have studied.

Hannah Carstairs is the main character in the historical novel *A Respectable Girl* written by Fleur Beale.

.... states title, author and main character

At the beginning of the novel Hannah is young, only 15 years old, living in New Plymouth in 1860, the time of land wars between British and Maori. Her mother died at 19 when she and her twin brother, Jamie, were born. She has a half brother, Arama, who is part Maori. She already carries domestic responsibilities in her family.

.... link to topic

In polite society in 1860s New Plymouth Hannah is expected to be unaware of the facts of life. The novel demonstrates this early on by describing how Hannah helps deliver a baby but is expected to hide this from society. 'It is something no respectable girl should even know about, let alone witness!' says Hannah's Aunt Frances. Hannah wants to be respectable but she also wants to know about things that matter so much to women.

.... supporting quotations from text

The novel shows how gradually Hannah learns about babies and their growth. Farming teaches about the practicalities of birth and she helps other mothers with too many children cope on a daily basis. Hannah, however, decides she will never marry as this means having babies and babies were a dangerous business, especially 'for a girl who could not believe in gooseberry bushes', as she thinks to herself. At the end of the novel Hannah falls in love and does marry but to a man who understands her feelings and helps her to learn about birth control.

.... shows how she changes

Hannah also has to think about the divisions between Maori and Pakeha when war begins, as her brothers are fighting on different sides. Although she admires the new settlers breaking in land and expanding the town, she believes 'buying' Maori land is wrong but as she is white she is expected to support the British. She runs away to England with her twin who has decided the only way he will not be obliged to fight his brother is by not being there at all. Hannah learns that some things she cannot change, and that seeing both sides of the question does not always help.

.... plot is told to show how main character learns life lessons

Hannah learns unpleasant things about her mother, that she and Jamie may be illegitimate, from gossip from a British soldier. Hannah tries to ignore this man but his taunting troubles her and she blames her dead mother. But when she goes to England to find her aristocratic father she discovers that her mother was married to him, so she has to rethink her attitude towards her mother. 'I breathed a prayer to Mama, pleading for forgiveness for my thoughts about her.'

.... paragraph link

.... quotations used throughout to support points made

Hannah learns how unpleasant it is to live where you are not loved, even if you are legitimate and from a wealthy family; where you are seen as a burden to be married off at the earliest opportunity. Alone in the family library she chooses to reread Jane Eyre. 'I wanted the familiar, I wanted comfort. I, like Jane, knew what it was to be unwanted and unwelcome.' She has to develop personal strength to deal with her situation and comes out of it stronger and more independent as she grows up quickly. She decides to return to New Zealand and shape a life for herself that is 'a useful one'.

Hannah Carstairs over the time during which this novel is set goes from a sturdily determined girl whose life is in reality fixed by society's attitudes about female status, to a young woman who chooses her own destiny. Her self-confidence and ability to rise above petty social prejudices grow and allow her to forge her own destiny.

.... conclusion links back to essay topic

1. Definition:

A **play** is a prose text, written in dialogue, designed to be performed / viewed rather than read. An essay about a play is a piece of literary criticism that analyses and evaluates the text.

2. Purpose and Role of Writer:

the playwright aims to entertain and, perhaps, convey a point of view; the writer of a drama essay aims to provide insight into the play by responding to a set question in a relevant and literate manner

3. Generic Features:

a) Structure and Organisation

- introduction names the text and its author and poses a hypothesis in response to a set question
- body: develops the hypothesis in a series of logically sequenced and relevant paragraphs
- conclusion: restates the hypothesis and sums up with a final evaluative comment e.g. *He persuades his audience ...*
- paragraph structure follows a set formula
  — topic sentences open paragraphs and signpost the argument e.g. *There is slapstick*
  — the body of the paragraph explains and elaborates on the opening sentence
  — each paragraph should provide examples or a quotation from the text e.g. *'Oh Glory!'*
  — the final sentence of the paragraph may clinch the argument

b) Language

- formal language
- literary terms e.g. *scene; plot; dialogue*
- linking words e.g. *Through; Also; and*
- conclusive words e.g. *a happy ending*

c) Grammar

- compound and complex sentences
- paragraph structure
- quotations from the text
- introduction, body, conclusion

Essay Question: The purpose of literature, especially drama, is to entertain an audience as well as to persuade it to a point of view. Is this a valid comment about a text you have studied?

The Playboy of the Western World by JM Synge is a 20th-century Irish drama that is both entertaining and persuasive. Set in pre-independence Ireland it entertains through its humour and vigorous characters and it persuades the audience to believe that the old Irish saying 'Praise youth and it will prosper' is true.

······ *introduction addresses key words of topic; states writer's approach to topic*

The play brings young Christy Mahon to a rural shebeen, the scene for the entire play. He is a stranger who tells a fine story, to Pegeen, a pretty but wild country girl who is to be married to timid, fat Shawn, whom she despises. Christy becomes the romantic hero, as Pegeen and the villagers believe his tales of his own exploits in the wide world beyond their experiences.

······ *main character named; literary term used*

······ *other characters named*

Christy claims to have killed his father and, while this is just a story, his tale is admired but when Old Mahon appears and Christy actually tries to murder him the scales fall away and the villagers now despise him. But the creature they created is alive and well and Christy realises he can stand up to his father and be a successful man.

······ *linking words*

Through Christy's tale, the plot shows the audience that if someone is praised and encouraged he can change his life and become the success he wants to be.

······ *play's point of view*

The play tells this tale for the most part with great humour. We can laugh when Christy's tale grows in elaborate detail as he gains confidence. Looking in a mirror he says: 'Didn't I know rightly, I was handsome, though it was the divil's own mirror we had beyond, would twist a squint across an angel's brow ...'

There is slapstick physical humour, as when Shawn is afraid to look after Pegeen overnight and loses his coat to the older men taunting him while escaping. Also when Christy is growing in confidence talking just to Pegeen but jumps in terror when someone knocks at the door:

······ *linking words*

> CHRISTY: It's time surely and I a seemly fellow with great strength in me and bravery of ... *(Someone knocks)*
>
> CHRISTY: *(clinging to PEGEEN)* Oh Glory! It's late for knocking and this last while I'm in terror of the peelers.

······ *use of quotation*

The characters' dialogue is full of lively religious imagery: 'Oh St Joseph, St Patrick, St Bridget and St James have mercy on me now!' begs Shawn. As he leaves at the end of the play Christy says: 'Ten thousand blessings on all that's here, for you've turned me a likely gaffer in the end of all, the way I'll go romancing through a romping lifetime from this hour to the dawning of the judgment day.'

······ *further reference to entertaining element*

JM Synge has created a realistic but comic celebration of peasant life through expressive graphic language and humorous characters. He persuades his audience that the saying 'Praise youth and it will prosper' is true as Christy gets a happy ending, becoming the confident man he wanted to be.

······ *conclusion; key ideas restated*

Structure

1. Definition:

A review is an analysis or appreciation of the quality of a live performance of a play.

2. Purpose and Role of Writer:

to inform and persuade / criticise

3. Generic Features:

a) Structure and Organisation

- introduction:
  — a combination of title, author and director; main actors
  — details theatre, time, dates and cost of performance
  — needs an angle / general opinionative comment e.g. *Another Willy Russell classic*
- brief plot analysis and speculation on the ending of the play
- ending not revealed
- analysis of key aspects of the play in a paragraph for each
  — key narrative techniques include: theme, plot, genre, characters, setting
    e.g. *not a very original basis for a plot; musical drama; set is minimalist*
  — key dramatic features include: acting, costumes, sets, sound, lighting
  — offer opinions of the quality of these aspects as you write e.g. *particularly appealing; suits the genre; actors are competent; standout performances*
- use some key quotes from the script
- provide some background on the playwright and the origin of the play
- make comparisons with other plays by the playwright, or in the same genre
- evaluate the expertise of the director and compare with other plays if possible
  e.g. *Another triumph*
- write in columns, in detail according to the word limit

b) Language

- formal
- literary language / the language of dramatic performance
- informative and opinionative e.g. *This creates humour, which balances well*
- impersonal language is the safe option e.g. *The tragic ending leaves the audience*

c) Grammar

- correct English necessary
- sentence fragments used for emphasis
- first person acceptable in moderation, but not necessary
- second person addressing the reader acceptable, but not necessary
- present tense

Blood Brothers
By Willy Russell
Directed by John Dayton
Caxton Theatre
20th June – 5th July

practical information about the production

More Bloody than Brotherly

catchy headline uses alliteration to summarise the play

Another Willy Russell classic is coming to the Caxton. Following hard on the success of *Educating Rita* is Russell's most famous play, a musical drama. Twins Mickey and Eddie are separated at birth as Mickey's mother, Mrs Johnson, cannot afford to bring up two more children. Persuaded by her rich but childless employer, she reluctantly parts with Edward, but the two boys are brought up in the same town, albeit very differently. Inevitably, they meet as teenagers and this is where the trouble begins.

background about the playwright / general plot outline but withholding the ending

While not a very original basis for a plot, the play does develop in an interesting way and end very dramatically. Both boys are very much a product of their environment. Mickey (Sean Jackson) is streetwise and a natural leader, whereas Edward (David Hamilton) is a naive and spoilt only child. Naturally, they both fall for the same girl, Linda (Natalie Parsons).

opinionative topic sentence opens the paragraph / insight into character

What makes this production particularly appealing in Act 1, especially, is the use of the adult actors dressed as children in oversized clothing with smuts on their faces and dirt on their clothes. This creates humour, which balances well with the later seriousness of the plot. The actors are competent in their roles, with standout performances by the charismatic Mickey who is idolised by his soppier twin, and by Eve Douglas as Mrs Lyons, Edward's 'mother' with her patronising manner and irritating social graces.

opinionative topic sentence / evaluation of the actors

The set is minimalist, but this suits the genre of the musical drama very well. The audience will enjoy the music as well as the drama, as all the actors have been selected for their vocal as well as their acting talents. The issues of social class and nature versus nurture emerge in the play as well as a warning about deception and taking the law into your own hands. The tragic ending leaves the audience with much to think about. Another triumph for John Dayton.

opinionative topic sentence / general conclusion about issues / final sentences encourage readers to see the play

Julie Turner

1. Definition:

A **play script** is the text or written version of a play.

2. Purpose and Role of Writer:

to entertain or to present a point of view about an issue or human nature in general

3. Generic Features:

a) Structure and Organisation

- play script divided into scenes and acts
- written in dialogue e.g. *What ... are you doing here?*
- stage directions included to describe movement, gesture, facial expression and interaction between characters e.g. *(rubbing her eyes sleepily)*
- plot involves conflict between and/or within characters e.g. *Help you? I'm taking you home right now!*
- number of characters restricted by stage performance
- physical setting also limited due to staging

b) Language

- dialogue to suit the social and cultural context of the play as well as the characters' ages, genders, personalities, plus the social and historical setting / social and cultural context of the play
- language may include colloquialisms, slang, expletives, according to the type of characters portrayed and the audience to which it is pitched e.g. *Bloody hell!*

c) Grammar

- emphasis on realism rather than grammatical correctness
- sentence fragments
- all tenses can be used
- first, second or third person

d) Delivery

- be sure that you understand the plot, your character and relationships with others
- enunciate clearly and speak loudly if on a stage
- apt vocal expression is vital to being a convincing actor
- plan your movements and facial expression to match the text
- be confident

The Stowaway

Scene 3: An isolated rural property in the backblocks .... setting is described in the script

In trouble with her mother, Angie has decided to run away from home. The perfect opportunity comes when she sees the van belonging to a fisherman she and her brother have been talking to on the beach. She slides the side door open and climbs in, hiding herself under a blanket. Minutes later, unaware of her presence, he climbs into the driver's seat and heads for his home in the nearby hills.

.... title gives a clue to the plot

.... background information: the story so far

Frank: *(sliding the door of his van open, noting a lump underneath the blanket)* What's this? *(He pulls the blanket off.)* What ... are you doing here?

.... stage directions indicate movement

Angie: *(rubbing her eyes sleepily)* Hello. Where am I?

Frank: *(angrily)* Never mind that. What are you doing in my van? And where's your brother?

.... speeches are usually short interchanges
.... stage directions indicate mood

Angie: *(looking up at him)* Felix is gone. *(She bursts into tears.)*

Frank: Gone. You mean gone home, like you should have done. Not hidden in my van. You wanna get me into trouble?

.... dialogue creates atmosphere and suspense / vocabulary establishes character / language suits the situation

Angie: *(thoughtfully, drying her eyes)* No, mister, but you have to help me.

Frank: *(glaring at her)* Help you? I'm taking you home right now!

.... conflict develops as the scene progresses

Angie: *(terrified)* No! My mother'll kill me! Oh, please, mister. *(then defiantly)* I won't tell you my address.

Frank: The police station then. Come on. Let's go!

Angie: No! You have to help me! You have to!

Frank: Why should I help you? You're a stowaway. Get in the front. And put your seat belt on. *(He begins to close the side door of the van.)*

.... character traits emerge as the plot develops

Angie: *(desperately)* No, wait! Not the police! Take me to my dad's house. Please ...

Frank: Where does he live?

.... simple everyday language forms a realistic interchange between characters / informal spoken language is used in drama

Angie: Christchurch.

Frank: Christchurch? That's hundreds of kilometres away. Are you mad? Why should I take you there?

Angie: *(slowly, looking at him seriously)* Because if you don't take me to Christchurch, I'll tell the police you kidnapped me ... and Felix.

.... Angie's character becomes calculating and threatening

Frank: Felix! Where is Felix?

Angie: I don't know. I think he's lost.

Frank: *(burying his face in his hands)* Bloody hell! He's not the only one.

.... scene ends on a note of tension and suspense

1. Definition:

An **essay about poetry** demonstrates knowledge of and insight into a literary text.

2. Purpose and Role of Writer:

an academic essay that informs the reader by developing and proving a hypothesis in response to a set question

3. Generic Features:

a) Structure and Organisation

- introduction: names the text and its author and poses a hypothesis
  e.g. *it creates a clear picture*

- body: develops the hypothesis in a series of logically sequenced paragraphs

- conclusion: restates the hypothesis and sums up with a final evaluative comment

- paragraph structure follows a set formula
  — topic sentences are the opening sentences of each paragraph
    e.g. *In the third verse, the metaphor ...*
  — the body of the paragraph is an explanation or elaboration of the general opening statement
  — each paragraph should then provide examples from the text being analysed, or a quotation from the text, which may go beyond the end of a line of the poem
    e.g. *triple pain/spreading out in grass ripples*
  — final sentence concludes this aspect of the essay and may provide a link to the next paragraph e.g. *these symbols represent death*

b) Language

- formal language

- literary terms e.g. *imagery; verse; poet*

- figurative language e.g. *metaphor; simile; alliteration*

- linking words e.g. *then; goes on; another*

c) Grammar

- paragraph structure

- quotations from the text

- complex sentences likely

Roadside crosses

Not the worst roads have them. Ditches
are favourites, sometimes a tree
a stretch grown familiar, fatally.

And now the crosses have them. Plain
or named and draped with flowers, real
or artificial, hung by heels like fowls.

Sometimes a threesome, triple pain
spreading out in grass ripples
sometimes a single, special agony.

Drive carefully say the signs. *Slow down.*
But most of these crosses suggest someone ran
towards a ditch or upwards to a bank.

Not deliberately. The terrain is usually easy
with just a faint mishap, a possibility
the crosses, like tiny wayside chapels, complete.

By Elizabeth Smither

**Essay Question: Assess the effectiveness of the poem
in the way it depicts a particular scene.**

Model answer:

Roadside crosses is an effective poem because it creates a clear
picture in the reader's mind through the use of imagery and focuses
the reader's thoughts through sentence and verse structure.

*introduction uses key words
from the question;
shows understanding of the
purpose of poetry;
uses poetic terms*

The poem describes the crosses along roads, which mark the place of
a fatal accident. It begins with a negative 'Not', an unusual sentence
structure to make the reader stop and think about meaning. It then
gives three reasons why accidents happen: ditches, trees, and over-
familiarity, and then places the word 'fatally' at the end of the verse,
alone, after the comma, for emphasis. Repetition of verse structure
at the beginning and end of the poem, 'Not the worst' and 'Not
deliberately', is how the poet reminds the reader that these are minor
accidents but they have major consequences.

*subject and meaning of
poem is identified; syntax is
commented on; individual
significant words are isolated
and effect is described*

Smither chooses the verb 'draped' to describe the flowers on the
crosses, a delicate word that reminds the reader of coffins which are
often described as 'draped with flowers'. She goes on to use the simile
'hung by heels like fowls', another image to remind the reader that
these symbols represent death.

*vocabulary choice is further
identified and effect described;
figurative language also
identified and discussed*

In the third verse, the metaphor 'triple pain/spreading out in grass
ripples' creates a vivid simple image of three crosses and suggests the
expanding impact of these three deaths. The painful effect of what the
cross represents, 'sometimes a single, special agony', is emphasised
here with the use of alliteration.

*progress through the poem is
used to locate this paragraph
and images are discussed*

In the final verse, Smither, in a simile, compares the crosses to 'tiny
wayside chapels', places to make a passerby ponder and be wary of
the possibility of making a similar simple mistake while driving.

In *Roadside crosses*, the poet depicts a familiar scene, and by using
carefully selected and carefully arranged language emphasises for the
reader how easily such 'mishaps', in essence just bad luck, can have
such enormously sad and cautionary consequences.

*conclusion shows link between
poet's purpose and the
techniques used*

1. Definition:

A **Reference List**, at the end of an essay or article or book, states in detail all sources of information that have been used by a writer to complete his or her work.

Footnotes on each page can also be used to state sources of information.

A Bibliography is very similar but it lists just author, title and publishing details.

2. Purpose and Role of Writer:

- to acknowledge all sources of information used
- to give reader other sites for further information

3. Generic Features:

- A Reference List must be painstakingly accurate
- There are several ways to organise a Reference List but this is a straightforward one

  1. Start a new page at the end of your essay.
  2. Use the title **REFERENCES** or **REFERENCE LIST**
  3. For each source of information you need to provide:

a) Author's Name

- Surname, comma, initial/s followed by full stop e.g. *Cryer, M.*
- More than one author? Use commas to separate their names and an *ampersand* (&) to indicate their joint work: e.g. *Smith, W.P., & Jones, A.*
- If the reference is an edited book then put Ed. or Eds in brackets: e.g. *Mills, M., & Fisher, P. (Eds)*

b) Title of Book or Article

- Copy the title carefully. Use capital letters where the book or article does. Use italics for the title of a book. Put a comma before a page number but a full stop if no page number is listed. e.g. *The GODZONE DICTIONARY of favourite New Zealand words and phrases.*
- For an article in a magazine, do not use italics for the article, but do use them for the magazine's name: e.g. *Women's Weekly,* The Most Powerful Woman in the World?

c) Location of Quotations/Information

- Use the abbreviation p. for page. One page is p. More than one is pp. e.g. p. 87; pp. 23–25.

d) Publication Information

- The place of publication and the publisher's name need to be listed. Separate with a colon (:) and end with a full stop: e.g. Auckland, New Zealand: Random House.

e) Publication Date

- Put the latest publication date in brackets, after the title, followed by a full stop: e.g. (2014).

- A magazine or periodical will have a month, too. Write it in full: e.g. (October 2014).

f) How to reference web pages

- Use the same process of author, title, date and add the *URL* followed by a colon (:):

  e.g. Phillips, J., The New Zealand bush — What is the bush? Te Ara — the Encyclopedia of New Zealand (updated 13-July-2012). URL: http://www.TeAra.govt.nz/en/the-new-zealand-bush/page-1

Example

Putting it all together

- **a)** Cryer, M
- **b)** *The GODZONE DICTIONARY of favourite words and phrases*
- **c)** p. 31
- **d)** Auckland, New Zealand: Exisle Publishing
- **e)** (reprinted 2006).

Cryer, M., *The GODZONE DICTIONARY of favourite words and phrases*, p. 31. Auckland, New Zealand: Exisle Publishing (reprinted 2006).

1. Definition:

A **report** is an informative text written in an impersonal style.

2. Purpose and Role of Writer:

to inform or provide advice based on research undertaken on a specific topic

3. Generic Features:

a) Structure and Organisation

- cover page outlining title of report and author's name
- contents page detailing each numbered section of the report
- introduction explains the rationale (reasons the report has been commissioned) and its scope e.g. *Young drivers*
- body of the report outlines its findings in logical order
- conclusion makes general points as a result of the report and may include recommendations or solutions to problems discussed in the report

b) Language

- formal English e.g. *The total social cost*
- precise, factual and objective language e.g. *This is 24 percent*
- impersonal language e.g. *A high proportion of fatal crashes involving young drivers … occur on the open road.*

c) Grammar

- correct English
- complex sentences
- specialised terminology relating to the topic e.g. *primary responsibility; social cost; higher impact speed*
- present tense e.g. *Young drivers are more likely …*
- past tense e.g. *In 2012 young drivers aged 15–24 were involved*
- use of first person is inappropriate

From: NZ Ministry of Transport (extract)

Young drivers tend to be over-represented in all types of crashes. Young drivers are more likely to be involved in a crash than older drivers for the same time spent driving and the same distance driven.

> clear explanation of topic and parameters of report

In 2012 young drivers aged 15–24 were involved in 73 fatal traffic crashes, 549 serious injury crashes and 2,626 minor injury crashes. Of these crashes, the 15–24 year-old drivers had the primary responsibility[1] in 55 of the fatal crashes, 436 of the serious injury crashes and 2,044 of the minor injury crashes. These crashes resulted in 68 deaths, 567 serious injuries and 2,830 minor injuries.[2]

> presents general statistics first

> uses footnotes to flesh out / clarify terminology at end of report; this aids easy reading of report

The total social cost of the crashes in which 15–24 year-old drivers had the primary responsibility was $755 million. This is 24 percent of the social cost associated with all injury crashes.

> examines overall social cost of accidents

...

> indicates parts of report are left out.

... young drivers tend to be over-represented in all types of crash. Recent figures show that 15–19 year-old drivers make up just 5 percent of all licensed car drivers.[3] Yet, between 2010 and 2012, 15-19-year-old drivers accounted for 12 percent of all drivers involved in minor injury crashes, 11 percent of drivers in serious injury crashes, and 9 percent of drivers involved in fatal crashes.

> formal language

> may have an emphasis, e.g. 'just'

...

Of all young drivers (15–24 years old) involved in fatal crashes between 2010 and 2012, 78 percent were male. Males accounted for 69 percent of young drivers involved in serious injury crashes and 61 percent of those involved in minor injury crashes over the same period.

> statistics are presented accurately

A high proportion of fatal crashes involving young drivers (15–24 years old) occur on the open road. This is due to the typically high speeds on these roads, which results in higher impact speed if a crash occurs.

> reasoning indicated

---

1 The determination of primary responsibility for a crash is based on the crash movements and crash cause factors assigned in the Crash Analysis System. It is not based on legal liability or court conviction.
2 Definitions for fatal, serious and minor injuries and social cost are given in terminology at the end of the fact sheet.
3 The car licence population consists of drivers with full, restricted or learner car licences *(Motor Vehicle Crashes in New Zealand, 2012)*.

Read the whole report at
http://www.transport.govt.nz/research/crashfacts/youngdriverscrashfacts/

1. Definition:

A **research assignment** investigates a problem or a question, by referring to a variety of informative sources.

2. Purpose and Role of Writer:

to form a hypothesis and solve a problem or respond to a question by selecting and evaluating relevant information

3. Generic Features:

a) Structure and Organisation

(i) Plan: develop research questions

- key terms of the question? (WHAT?) e.g. *causes of World War I*
- key dates and places? (WHEN? WHERE?) e.g. *1871; 1914; France*
- key facts / events / examples / people? (WHAT? WHO? HOW?)
- key causes? (WHY?) e.g. *imperialism, nationalism, the arms race and a complex set of alliances between nations*
- key effects/ results/ changes? (WHAT?) e.g. *destabilising Europe*

(ii) Research and Reflection:

- take notes from a variety of primary and secondary sources
- reflect on the value of / organise this information according to the research questions above
- develop a hypothesis and state it clearly in your introduction, e.g. background and immediate cause resulted in a 'war climate'
- organise your information into logically developed paragraphs
- use topic sentences to signpost your argument e.g. *Another factor*
- use direct and indirect quotes to support your argument

(iii) Draft your response: in paragraphs using correct referencing of source material

(iv) Final Copy: an edited / corrected draft with correctly set out reference list (see pp. 56–57)

b) Language

- formal English
- specialised language according to topic e.g. *war climate; nationalism; imperialism*
- linking words e.g. *However; Another; Thus*
- clear, precise, unbiased language

c) Grammar

- correct paragraphing and punctuation
- complex sentences
- third person only e.g. *when war broke out, the ordinary man in the street*

***Assignment Task:* Outline the major causes of World War I**

The causes of the outbreak of World War I in 1914 are many and varied. There were background and immediate causes of what is called the Great War or 'the war to end all wars'. These included imperialism, nationalism, the arms race and a complex set of alliances between nations. A number of small conflicts arose that created a war climate in the early part of the twentieth century, making war seem inevitable.

> introduction states hypothesis 'many and varied', 'war … inevitable'; mentions a relevant date; lists the many causes; uses terminology, e.g. 'war climate'

Nationalism means loyalty and pride in one's country. Coupe (1981) states that as far as World War I is concerned, 'the fundamental causes can be traced back as far as the French and Economic Revolutions and the growth of nationalism, colonialism and economic rivalry which came with them'. Britain ruled a vast empire in this Victorian era. Germany and Italy were both unified into nation states in 1871, and their nationalistic feelings grew from this historic moment. France's nationalism grew from revenge and bitterness over the province of Alsace-Lorraine which Germany had taken by force in 1871. In the formerly powerful Austro-Hungarian Empire, there were many small ethnic groups who wanted self-determination, a chance to create their own separate nations.

> body develops the causes in turn; sample paragraph opens with a clear topic sentence; references quotes; develops the topic

…

Another factor that escalated nationalistic tensions was the press. Lawrence (1986) states that newspapers became a form of propaganda that built up feelings of aggressive nationalism termed jingoism, encouraging the population to feel that their nation was superior. Thus when war broke out, the ordinary man in the street was keen to enlist, even if he did not fully understand the conflict.

> sample paragraph: topic sentence uses a linking word; second reference is an indirect quote; final clincher sentence uses 'Thus' to indicate a concluding point

…

The immediate cause of World War I, the assassination of the Austrian Archduke Franz Ferdinand by a Bosnian student, released a 'powder keg' of aggressive feelings that had been simmering, ready to explode. However, this was just the culmination of other factors and rivalries that had been destabilising Europe for more than half a century.

> conclusion reinforces the original hypothesis; shows understanding of the topic; uses effective terminology and vocabulary

1. Definition:

Shakespearean drama describes the plays written by the English dramatist and poet, William Shakespeare (1564–1616). Shakespeare is regarded as the world's greatest playwright. His 37 plays included comedies, histories and, most famously, tragedies.

2. Purpose and Role of Writer:

to entertain / to present a message about human nature / to earn a living

3. Generic Features:

a) Structure and Organisation

- divided into five acts
- each act is subdivided into scenes
- first two acts represent the rising action of the play
- third act contains the climax
- final acts represent the falling action towards the resolution
- written in dialogue with few stage directions
- Shakespeare's plays feature characters of noble birth
- in tragedy, the central character — the tragic hero — is a man of virtue who, according to some scholars, contains a fatal flaw that leads to his downfall
- the plot of the play involves the reversal of his fortune, and at the end of the play all the major characters die; a new order prevails, creating hope for the future
- the play often features supernatural influences — ghosts or witches — that influence the plot

b) Language

- written in blank verse, arranged in lines of poetry
- Shakespeare is most famous for his metaphorical language
- some of the language is dated and difficult to understand
- most famous speeches are the soliloquies where the character is alone on stage expressing his feelings in monologue form

c) Grammar

- play written in sentences but in stanza form

Analysing Hamlet's soliloquy

Hamlet is a Shakespearean tragedy about a Danish prince who discovers that his Uncle Claudius has murdered his father, the king, and married his mother, Gertrude. The ghost of the dead king swears Hamlet to revenge his death. Hamlet, an honourable man, is confused and hovers between hatred and anger, and an inability to commit the murder of his uncle.

A soliloquy is a speech or monologue, delivered by the character when he is alone on stage. Its purpose is to reveal the character's thoughts and feelings, and to give some indication of the future action of the play. Below is Hamlet's fifth soliloquy.

Hamlet: 'Tis now the very witching time of night, ·········· reference to the supernatural
When churchyards yawn and hell itself breathes out ·········· personification
Contagion to this world: now could I drink hot blood, ·········· metaphor
And do such bitter business as the day ·········· alliteration
Would quake to look on. Soft! now to my mother.
O heart, lose not thy nature; let not ever
The soul of Nero enter this firm bosom: ·········· reference to ancient Roman history
Let me be cruel, not unnatural:
I will speak daggers to her, but use none; ·········· metaphor
My tongue and soul in this be hypocrites; ·········· personification
How in my words so ever she be shent,
To give them seals never, my soul, consent. ·········· rhyming couplet

Act III, Scene 2

Analysis of the soliloquy

In this soliloquy, Hamlet is reacting to the confirmation that his uncle is guilty of his father's murder. He is angry with Claudius and extremely revengeful. This is evident in the line 'now could I drink hot blood', an exaggerated example of the way Hamlet feels, which creates a dramatic atmosphere in the play.

The seven soliloquies that Hamlet delivers in the play are varied in tone and intent. This is evidence of his instability as a result of his father's death and mother's remarriage. Here Hamlet also expresses his revulsion for his mother, in her betrayal of his father's memory. He has been summoned to his mother's room to be rebuked for his behaviour. Instead, Hamlet will 'speak daggers' to Gertrude. Tempted though he is, he will not harm her physically.

The theme of this speech is obviously revenge. Shakespeare wanted to emphasise Hamlet's outrage and sense of duty to his father. He does this through metaphorical language and blank verse that create an atmosphere of tension and foreboding. As with most soliloquies, the final rhyming couplet creates a neat ending.

1. Definition:

An essay on **Shakespearean drama** demonstrates knowledge of and insight into a literary text.

2. Purpose and Role of Writer:

to write an academic essay that informs the reader by developing and proving a hypothesis in response to a set question

3. Generic Features:

a) Structure and Organisation

- introduction: names the text and its author and poses a hypothesis e.g. *It conforms closely*

- body: develops the hypothesis in a series of logically sequenced paragraphs

- conclusion: restates the hypothesis and sums up with a final evaluative comment e.g. *Thus, it can be seen that Hamlet*

- paragraph structure follows a set formula
  - topic sentences are the opening sentences of each paragraph e.g. *Shakespeare is famous*
  - the body of the paragraph is an explanation or elaboration of the general opening statement
  - each paragraph should then provide examples from the text being analysed, or a quote from the text e.g. *Claudius, the wicked uncle, contrasts with his brother*
  - the final sentence is a clincher that concludes this aspect of the argument and provides a link to the next paragraph

b) Language

- formal language

- literary terms e.g. *blank verse*

- linking words

- conclusive words e.g. *However; Therefore*

c) Grammar

- complex sentences

- paragraph structure

- quotations from the text e.g. *'O that this too too solid flesh would melt'*

Essay Question: Discuss the ways in which the play, *Hamlet*, conforms to the general characteristics of Shakespearean tragedy.

Hamlet is regarded by some critics as Shakespeare's finest tragedy. It conforms closely to the characteristics of all of Shakespeare's plays in this genre, being written in blank verse with a plot that traces a noble family and the reversal of fortune of the once noble hero by tracing his downfall. The plot juxtaposes good and evil characters — some of whom are supernatural — and has a message for people of all ages.

> introduction responds directly to the question by forming a hypothesis that develops four characteristics of the tragedy

It is important that the audience of a Shakespearean play empathises with the protagonist. Generally he is a character of noble birth and admirable qualities; until fate deals him a blow that changes his life forever. In *Hamlet*, the audience admires Hamlet's sense of duty to his father when he swears to revenge his murder. However, the audience also becomes impatient, as Hamlet delays fulfilling his pledge to his father.

> develops one of the four aspects outlined in the introduction, i.e. shows the two sides of the tragic hero that lead to his downfall

Although Shakespeare never left England, some of his plays are set in other countries. Hamlet is set in Elsinore, Denmark and the characters are the Danish royal family. This does not mean that all are virtuous characters. Claudius, the wicked uncle, contrasts with his brother the late king. Gertrude, the queen, has been depicted by Shakespeare as a weak character. Even Hamlet has some weaknesses, being very melancholy and indecisive: 'O that this too too solid flesh would melt'.

> develops a second aspect, i.e. noble birth

Shakespeare is famous for the timelessness and universality of his plays. Although his plots are extreme and somewhat unrealistic, the characters in his plays display complex human traits that are recognisable today, like ambition and vengeance. Hamlet describes his uncle as a 'remorseless, lecherous, treacherous villain'.

> develops a third aspect, i.e. universality; uses quote

The plots of Shakespeare's tragedies also follow a general pattern. The action in the first half of the play tends to be hopeful, despite some calamity. The tragic hero seems to be in control. The climax or turning point occurs in the middle of the play, generally with a revelation that will change the fortunes of the protagonist. In *Hamlet*, the confirmation of Claudius's guilt comes via a play within the play called *The Mousetrap*. From this point, Hamlet loses control of the action, thus allowing further tragedy to occur. At the end of the play, all major characters are dead as a result of 'carnal, bloody and unnatural acts'.

> develops a fourth aspect, i.e. plot

There are some characteristics of Shakespearean tragedy that are less acceptable in modern society, the presence of the supernatural, for example. It is the ghost of Hamlet's father who reveals the murder plot. Four hundred years ago, the people of Shakespeare's time believed in ghosts and other supernatural phenomena. Today, we are not so superstitious. Nor are we used to plays written in poetic form. Shakespeare wrote his plays in blank verse with liberal use of metaphorical language.

> introduces other minor aspects

Thus, it can be seen that *Hamlet* is typical of other Shakespearean tragedies, being the story of a potentially great man who is undermined by circumstance. In each of the tragedies, the main character dies, but there is always one character left to take over the kingdom, and restore order. Therefore, the tragedy ends on a positive note.

1. Definition:

A short story is a narrative of fewer than 20,000 words with a simple plot, a small number of characters and one setting. A short story can be read at one sitting.

2. Purpose and Role of Writer:

to entertain

3. Generic Features:

a) Structure and Organisation

- decide on a topic
- decide on a sub genre: crime, fantasy, mainstream narrative
- decide on the angle or theme, e.g. case of mistaken identity forms the twist
- decide on an appealing title
- plot the story with conflict, a crisis, a climax and a conclusion
- aim to create atmosphere through suspense
- conclusion may be a twist or unexpected ending e.g. *This was her final rehearsal*
- decide whether the story will have a traditional or alternative structure
- create characters: central character and one or two others if necessary
- decide on setting e.g. *They continued to sit in the semi-darkness*
- decide on first, second or third person method of narration e.g. *She*

b) Language

- language to suit the genre, era and social context of the story
- a blend of action, description, dialogue and reflection to create variety. This story has deliberately avoided using dialogue to create an atmosphere of silence and mystery.
- evocative language to create atmosphere e.g. *She swallowed nervously*
- figurative language in descriptions e.g. *Like shadows or slinky cats*

c) Grammar

- a variety of short and long sentences
- short sentences / fragments used for drama and impact
- a variety of sentence beginnings
- the correct conventions for writing dialogue
- correct paragraphing
- past and / or present tense, e.g. past tense for a past happening

Sometimes Silence Says It All

No one spoke. They continued to sit in the semi-darkness, watching. Sitting on the dusty floor, all were dressed in black. Some of the girls had taken the blackness to extremes, Sarah noted, dyeing their hair and wearing black stockings that disappeared up their slim legs under their short skirts. They were all emaciated looking, even the boys. It went with the territory. Like shadows or slinky cats, they moved around the room when they were summoned to take their turn.

Looking around restlessly, Sarah saw a tiny black spider weaving its web between the tattered curtains close to the narrow window at the side of the room. Like everything else in the cold building, the window was grimy. Outside, it was starting to drizzle and the sky was darkening prematurely. Sarah wished that she could slip through one of the cracks in the window unnoticed, even though it would be chilly outside.

It wasn't the silence that bothered her any more. She'd grown accustomed to reading facial expressions and the mood of the others' movements. To speak, even to whisper to Maura, the girl beside her, the redheaded girl with the freckles that looked like chocolate chips on her pale face, would be unforgivable. Sarah noticed that Maura was chewing her fingernails and staring blankly ahead. Must be psyching herself up.

Who could have imagined a group of teenagers could sit so silently and so still? They'd certainly learned some discipline lately. It was like being reprogrammed, becoming robotic. To speak would be like laughing out loud in church. She shuddered at the thought.

Pulling the dark shawl closer to her chest, Sarah fixed her eyes on the pale young man in front of her. He was edging his way along the side wall as if he too wanted to escape through the nearby exit. His movements were furtive but fluid, like a dancer performing to some distant music that only he could hear. Then he melted back into the group, seating himself silently.

Suddenly, Sarah was beckoned forward. She swallowed nervously, hiding her shaking hands behind her back. By the time she reached the front of the room, she felt her nerves begin to calm. It wasn't as if she had to remember any lines. There was no need to speak. It was movement and facial expression that were crucial. This was her final rehearsal at the famous Marcel Marceau School of Mime, and Sarah was about to give the most important performance of her acting career so far. She began her well practised routine. Conscious that all the eyes in the room were upon her, Sarah enveloped herself in the silence, pleased that the ordeal would soon be over. No one spoke.

Marginal annotations:

- title hints at the content of the story
- introduction sets the scene visually and identifies the main character and the action / language creates atmosphere
- focus on the main character.
- third person narrative looks through main character's eyes / becomes reflective
- use of rhetorical question / emphasis on atmosphere
- verbs and adjectives create visual images of the scene / figurative language
- story approaches climax and revelation of purpose as it focuses on the central character
- final sentence is a repetition of the opening

1. Definition:

A song is a poem that can be sung.

2. Purpose and Role of Writer:

to entertain or to arouse an emotional reaction

3. Generic Features:

a) Structure and Organisation

- topic: is often love or relationships
- theme: is often sad about lost or unrequited love
- title: sums up the message of the poem
- structure: stanza form, usually with a chorus
- generally regular stanza length; quatrains are common

b) Language

- emotive words associated with love e.g. *alone; haunts; faithful*
- language creates dramatic atmosphere
- use of figurative devices like those used in poetry
  - simile: e.g. *My life's like a nightmare*
  - metaphor: e.g. *The world is your oyster / Let me be your pearl*
- Use of question form: e.g. *Why can't you love me? / Why won't you stay?*
- Rhyme: regular rhyme scheme: e.g. *name / same; away / day*

c) Grammar

- written in lines, but in sentence form
- line divisions indicate pauses and create rhythm
- punctuation is used according to sentence division
- syntax (word order) may be varied as in poetry

Love Whisper

When I'm alone I **whisper your** name ⋯⋯⋯⋯ emotive, personal language / use of first person
I still can't believe you don't feel the same
The love that we shared: it won't fade away
I know I'll love you, till my dying day

My life's like a nightmare
that haunts me each day ⋯⋯⋯⋯ simile/ dramatic mood / question form
Why can't you love me?
Why won't you stay?

The world is your oyster
Let me be your pearl ⋯⋯⋯⋯ metaphors
I'll always be faithful
Your one and only girl

All I want is a chance
to prove that I can
love you forever;
you don't understand ⋯⋯⋯⋯ emotive language

Let bygones be bygones
Let's start anew — please!
You know I still want you ⋯⋯⋯⋯ repetition of words
You know I'll be true

Remember the good times
the love we both shared?
Those halcyon days ⋯⋯⋯⋯ development of emotional mood
when you showed that you cared.

I'm writing this letter
please listen to me
I've tried and I've tried
but I can't shake you free

When I'm alone I whisper your name
I still can't believe you don't feel the same
The love that we shared: it won't fade away
I know I will love you, love you, love YOU! ⋯⋯⋯ repetition of chorus as the song builds to an
Till my dying day. emotional crescendo

1. Definition:

An **occasional speech** is one made to friends or relatives on an important occasion, like a rite of passage, e.g. 18th birthday, marriage or funeral.

2. Purpose and Role of Writer:

to celebrate or commemorate a significant occasion

3. Generic Features:

a) Structure and Organisation

- introduction
  - should give background information / a clear explanation of the topic
    e.g. *a quiet, modest and self-effacing man*
  - could begin with an anecdote that is symbolic of the person or situation
- body of the speech should introduce highlights of a person's life or significant details that develop the reason for the speech e.g. *family; school; work; war*
- conclusion should sum up and finish strongly e.g. *Grandad was a real family man*
- leave the audience with a strong impression, or something memorable
  e.g. *Goodbye, Grandad; we'll miss you.*

b) Language

- language choice / degree of formality depends on occasion and audience
- a eulogy may be formal in language or informal if the purpose is to uplift or cheer the audience e.g. *He also fulfilled his ambition to become an engineer*
- even though the occasion may be serious, the speaker still required to entertain / hold the audience's attention e.g. *He had lied about his age*
- language and structure to be sufficiently simple and clear to allow listeners to follow the theme and text of the speech

c) Grammar

- correct grammar is important
- sentence fragments are acceptable e.g. *That's because*

d) Delivery

- delivery as important as the text
- speak slowly and deliberately
- be enthusiastic / respectful and sincere
- maintain as much eye contact with your audience as possible
- stand still
- limit gestures so that the audience is not distracted

Eulogy

Family and friends

If my grandfather, John Smith, were here today he would be amazed by the number of people seated in front of me. That's because he was such a quiet, modest and self-effacing man. Grandad never wanted to be the centre of attention, as he is today.

> establishes speaker's relationship with deceased; makes a general thematic statement

John Smith was born in 1922 on a property outside Duntroon, near Oamaru. He grew up in a carefree atmosphere, riding horses and helping with the sheep on the property. He loved the countryside. Sadly, when the Great Depression came in 1929, the Smith family was forced to sell their property cheaply, and move to Dunedin.

> background information includes dates and places, emphasising key positives and negatives and points of interest

Because Grandad was the eldest child of six in the family, he was forced to leave school at the age of fourteen, even though he was a clever boy who wanted to be an engineer. Until he was seventeen, John worked in a local bakery, rising at 3 a.m. in order to help with the baking of the bread, which he would sell to local customers when the bakery opened at 7 a.m. These were long hours and the work was nonstop.

> continues the personal history in a chronological style

Grandad often told us that he was glad when war broke out in 1939. Like so many men of the time, he saw it as an opportunity for overseas travel and adventure. Grandad was put in the Catering Corps, which he didn't think much of. He had lied about his age to get into the army as he was only seventeen, and he was determined to see some action. When Grandad returned after the war, he married Anne, his childhood sweetheart. He also fulfilled his ambition to become an engineer, after finishing high school and winning an ex-serviceman's scholarship.

> emphasises rites of passage, high and low points and links to history

Grandad was a real family man. He loved nothing better than the Christmas holidays spent with his extended family at Blueskin Bay, north of Dunedin. He taught us to body surf and always loved our games of beach cricket. He also loved spending time with friends, playing bowls or bridge or just enjoying a beer and a chat. Above all, Grandad was lucky to live a long and healthy life and to be released from it without a great deal of pain or suffering. Goodbye, Grandad; we'll miss you.

> conclusion becomes more general and contains some personal referents

1. Definition:

A **persuasive speech** aims to convince an audience about a particular issue through factual evidence.

2. Purpose and Role of Writer:

to deliver a well-written script in a persuasive manner

3. Generic Features:

a) Structure and Organisation

- opening should
  - — arouse interest through an example, quote or general statement
    e.g. *Do we have any self-made millionaires in the room today?*
  - — opening should make speaker's point of view clear e.g. *Your principal has invited me here to talk to you today about money*
- each paragraph should build upon the argument logically
  - — topic sentences should be used as signposts e.g. *Saving is one answer*
  - — arguments should be supported by examples / statistics / quotes
    e.g. *In three weeks you'll be leaving school*
  - — include rebuttal of the opposing viewpoint
- conclusion should be strong and persuasive e.g. *live for today, but keep the future firmly in mind*

b) Language

- formal and correct English to create an air of authority and expertise
- persuasive but not overly emotive e.g. *Think for a moment*
- language must suit age and educational level of audience e.g. *cool to eat in the uni cafe*
- vocabulary must include the terminology of the topic e.g. *fixed interest rates; superannuation*
- language must be simplified for a listening audience

c) Grammar

- short or carefully punctuated sentences for a listening audience
- use exclamations and hypothetical questions for dramatic effect
  e.g. *A car? A house? A mortgage?*
- use the second person pronoun — *you* — to address audience directly
  e.g. *You're probably sick*
- use the first person plural — *we* — to include the audience in the argument

d) Delivery

- verbal features: speak slowly and clearly, enunciate carefully, vary vocal expression, check pronunciation. Rehearse before final delivery to familiarise yourself with your material.
- nonverbal features: stand straight, don't move about, limit hand gestures. Look enthusiastic about your topic and show interest in your audience. Radiate confidence and conviction. Maintain eye contact with everyone in the audience.

Good morning, Year 13, ···|··· greeting

Do we have any self-made millionaires in the room today? **No, I thought not. Put your hand up please if you have a part-time job. That's good, as long as it doesn't interfere with your studies. I'm John Moneypenny, a financial adviser at BGT Limited, one of the largest and most successful financial institutions in the country.** Your principal has invited me here to talk to you today about money: **how to save it, how to make it and how to make it work for you.**

······ introduction aims to hook audience through rhetorical question / contextualises speech

In three weeks you'll be leaving school **and entering the adult world. For some of** you, **this will mean enrolling at university and others will go straight into the workforce. Most of you will be living at home. But not forever.** I'm sure you all want **to be independent as soon as possible. This means planning for the future.**

······ use of second person

You're probably sick of hearing about how the exchange rate has affected the lives of ordinary New Zealanders, **and how your life will be more difficult financially than that of your parents. Unfortunately, this is a fact for most of you. This is why you need to plan.** Think for a moment **where you'd like to be in ten or twelve years' time. Finish this sentence in your mind. By the time I'm thirty, I want to have these assets. I want ...**

······ addresses the audience directly and involve them in order to persuade

A car? A house? A mortgage? (No one really wants a mortgage, but ···|··· more rhetorical questions
we **all have them if we're smart.) An overseas trip? Now think about how you're going to achieve these things, and later on provide for your children's education and their demands on your wallet.**

Saving is one answer. You need to learn to budget. **Allocate money where you need it. Don't be mean to yourself but keep the books balanced. It may be** cool to eat in the uni cafe, **but a packed lunch eaten in the uni gardens is probably more nutritious and certainly cheaper. Public transport is a better option than driving to work or uni for most people, especially if you advance purchase your tickets. It all comes down to being organised and thinking ahead.**

······ short sentences / examples of ways to save

Some of you are studying business subjects already. **You probably know about** fixed interest rates **for banks and the need to shop around to make your dollars spread further. You may even have ventured into the stock market. Non-business students need to understand how the financial system works.**

······ appeal to a section of the audience

Those of you going into the workforce need to get the best from your superannuation **from the outset of your career.** Look into the **value of contributing extra funds to your super.** Keep up **those part-time jobs, those of you who are continuing your studies, and keep an up-to-date résumé to make yourself as marketable as possible.**

······ use of imperatives

Finally, Year 13: live for today, but keep the future firmly in mind. ······ conclusion is brief but dramatic
Know where you're heading and how you're going to get there. Good luck!

1. Definition:

A **textual intervention** is a creative response to a text, adding to the story or filling a gap or a silence.

2. Purpose and Role of Writer:

to show an understanding of the content of the text and to recreate the style of the author

3. Generic Features:

a) Structure and Organisation

- intervention is a prelude, interlude or postlude text e.g. *The action takes place at the end of Chapter 1*
- conforms to the original text in layout and development
- may be a chapter or a part of a chapter
- text must flow smoothly from the original and back to the original

b) Language

- must be consistent with the original text e.g. *I like dogs because they don't talk and confuse me.*
- must show features of the original text e.g. *The walls of the cell were blue*
- must use vocabulary consistent with the original text
- may be formal or informal e.g. *I was in the cell at the police station*

c) Grammar

- may be first, second or third person e.g. *I didn't feel tired; I wasn't even hungry*
- may be present or past tense e.g. *I liked being alone*
- may be grammatically correct or not
- sentence fragments may be used

The following is a textual intervention based on the novel *The Curious Incident of the Dog in the Night-Time* by Mark Haddon, about a boy with Asperger's syndrome. The action takes place at the end of Chapter 1.

I was in the cell at the police station for 47 minutes and 23 seconds. I didn't know what would happen next so I sat down on the padded bench and waited.

> use of statistics to show character's precise nature

The walls of the cell were blue, with some large white chips out of the paintwork near the floor. It looked like someone had kicked the wall because there were shoe marks there too. It reminded me of the sky and the clouds because of the colours. My teacher would probably ask me to write a simile about it, if she was in the room. But I don't like similes. I don't understand them, especially the really weird ones in the poetry we sometimes read. I don't like poetry. I like nonfiction books with lots of facts. But because the sky was blue on a fine day, I felt comfortable in the police cell.

I liked being alone. It gave me plenty of time to think about what had happened. I know now that Mrs Shears called the police. She thinks I killed Wellington. I know that now because when she came out onto the front lawn in her pyjamas, I was holding on to Wellington and she swore at me. So many times, people don't understand me. I was trying to save Wellington. But it was too late. He was already dead. Like my mother.

> reference to solitary nature of character

Mrs Shears knows I like Wellington. Dogs are a lot more intelligent than some people. I like dogs because they don't talk and confuse me. I don't like people touching me, but I don't mind dogs jumping up on me because I know that means they want to be patted. When people touch me, I don't know what they want. That's why I hit the policeman. That's why I'm sitting here.

> first person, past tense / reflection on past events to orientate the reader

It was nice and cool in the police cell. At 12.34, one of the officers looked in at me. He opened the hatch and nodded. I didn't know what that meant so I ignored him. I didn't feel tired. I like night-time because it's quiet and everyone else is in bed. I wasn't even hungry. I thought about my pet rat, Toby. I wondered if he was asleep. If he was awake, he would be hungry. I always give him a snack before I put him into his cage at night.

> shows knowledge of character's feelings about dogs / more emotional detachment

I was just thinking about how the room was perfectly symmetrical when I heard voices. Nobody came, so I started to think about the death of Wellington. When I get home I am going to make a list of suspects and a plan for how I will solve the crime. Then Mrs Shears will be pleased. Mrs Shears knows I always tell the truth. She didn't ask me if I knew who killed Wellington, so I didn't tell her. I will find out for her, for Wellington really. Then if Mrs Shears gets another dog, she will let me take him for a walk.

> sentence structure — use of 'I' to show character's self-centredness / reference to the shape of the room shows another aspect of the character / more reference to the plot of the novel

'What the bloody hell's going on?' I recognised that voice echoing down the corridor.

> ends on a note of suspense

---

1. Definition:

A **textual reconstruction** changes or reconstructs some aspect/s of a text, often in a different genre.

2. Purpose and Role of Writer:

to show an understanding of a text by responding to it creatively, generally reinforcing, but sometimes resisting the meaning of the original text

3. Generic Features:

a) Structure and Organisation

- choose a part of the text where the story can be reconstructed

- choose an appropriate genre for the reconstruction e.g. narrative, feature article

- if the narrative genre is used, there should be a balance of action, narrative, dialogue, description and reflection e.g. *Now he feels vulnerable*

- a reconstruction can be a fragment or an episode, a 'small picture'; does not have to cover the whole text; e.g. the text ends abruptly as the doctor arrives.

b) Language

- language must
  - — suit the plot, characters and setting of your reconstruction
  - — could vary from formal to informal, depending on its purpose
    e.g. *'So who's this Dr Freud anyway?'*
  - — suit the chosen genre.

- consistent person and tense throughout the text e.g. third person: *Hamlet; he*

- apply the rules of narrative writing or the genre chosen to the text; refer to the rules that apply to other text types elsewhere in this writing guide

This textual reconstruction has transformed *Hamlet* by William Shakespeare into a modern setting. Hamlet has been acting strangely since his father's mysterious death and his mother's remarriage to an uncle whom he detests. Is Hamlet mad or sad? To find out, his mother plans to have him see a psychoanalyst.

'What's this?' Hamlet bursts into his mother's room without knocking. He's holding a piece of paper in his hand.

········· dialogue creates mood, establishes modern setting, begins plot

'It's a referral, Hamlet, to a specialist. I made the appointment for you,' his mother, Gertrude, replies, startled by his abrupt and noisy entry. She's sitting in her favourite chair by the window, reading. Now she places her book on the window ledge.

········· establishes setting, creating visual effect

'So who's this Dr Freud anyway?' Hamlet paces across the room restlessly as Gertrude watches him closely.

········· insight into character

'He's an eminent psychologist, Hamlet,' Gertrude replies, an anxious tone in her voice. 'You need a doctor. You're sick, even if you don't realise it.'

········· creates mood

'Sick? What am I suffering from?' Hamlet's voice rises in anger. He turns to face her. 'Well?'

········· creates conflict, suspense

Gertrude stands and moves towards him warily. She seems almost afraid to speak. 'Look at yourself in the mirror,' she urges him. 'You've been wearing the same black clothes for six months now, and they're hanging off you.'

········· link to original text

'You mean I'm anorexic, or I just have bad fashion sense. Black is the "in" colour this year. It's just that you haven't noticed, Mother. You've been too busy since my father's death.' Turning from the full-length mirror, he moves towards her, gripping her hands and pulling her closer. 'Look at yourself for a moment,' he commands. 'My father's been dead for five minutes and you look like you're going to a party.' Hamlet points to the new hot-pink dress his mother is wearing. 'It's embarrassing.'

········· insight into character

Gertrude sighs. 'Your father died more than six months ago, Hamlet. This is what I mean. You need help. You've changed so much.'

········· link to original plot

Hamlet moves to the window. He looks out at the view of the wild Danish sea that he used to love so much. His life used to be predictable. Now he feels vulnerable, like the coastline below, buffeted by the waves that crash over it incessantly.

········· reflection, figurative language, link to original plot

Just as he is tempted to push the window open and fling himself out, and maybe take his mother with him, there is a knock on the door. A small dark-haired man is being ushered into the room. 'Ah,' Hamlet says, smiling slightly. 'You must be Dr Fraud, my new shrink.'

········· insight into character

'Freud,' his mother corrects him. 'Welcome, Dr Freud. This is my son, Hamlet.'

········· lacks conclusion, ends on an uncertain note

1. Definition:

Online texts are types of written communication on the world wide web, which form part of the internet. These texts include a vast amount of information that is accessible through web browsers and then refined through search engines such as Google. The homepage is the opening page of a website, which introduces the visitor to the purpose and features of the site.

2. Purpose and Role of Writer:

to provide information, to advertise and to sell products

3. Generic Features:

a) Structure and Organisation

- written and visual information are both designed to attract the eye
- information is arranged in small readable sections
- visual content may dominate
- individual websites vary in text and layout but conform to a general pattern or style

b) Language

- may be formal or informal according to the subject of the website
- generally persuasive language
- language specific to the subject of the website may be used
- language to appeal to a certain age, gender, interest group may be used
- language specific to online communities may be used

c) Grammar

- generally correct language use
- may involve the reader with personal pronouns you / we / our
- imperatives may be used
- sentence fragments may be used

heading is company title | menu to navigate site | lively visual used to interest and engage reader (the real one scrolls across, too!)

Foodstuffs NZ

Site search 🔍

🏠 | WORKING AT FOODSTUFFS | FOODSTUFFS CO-OPERATIVE | STORES & SERVICES | FEATURED ROLES | SEARCH FOR JOBS

Welcome

Welcome to the world of Foodstuffs. Our aim is to make life better – for you and for our customers. A career with Foodstuffs is about enjoyment, challenge, rewards, and adding value to life. Take your time, look around, and discover what Foodstuffs can do for you.

Our Brands

Putting faces to names! Discover the household names that are our Foodstuffs brands. **More »**

Stores & Services

Wherever you work in the world of Grocery and Fresh Foods, there's always something happening. **More »**

LIKE WHAT YOU SEE?

Discover the world of career opportunities waiting for you at Foodstuffs.

Job Search

MEET OUR PEOPLE

See Foodstuffs through the eyes of the people driving the business.

Watch Videos

persuasive language | imperatives | rhetorical question | personal pronouns to engage reader

1. Definition:

A **weblog**, sometimes written as *web log* or *Weblog*, more commonly known as a **blog**, a website that consists of a series of entries arranged in reverse chronological order, often updated frequently with new information about particular topics.

2. Purpose and Role of Writer:

- to share the writer's thoughts and feelings, ideas, opinions

- to describe life events

- to share school projects and homework!

- to develop a commentary on a theme, by one or several people

- to persuade readers to purchase a particular product or brand

3. Generic Features:

a) Structure and Organisation

- a title related to the purpose of the blog e.g. *quad bike to quad-copter*

- photo of author and/or photo related to theme of blog

- a central column of text and photos

- side columns, which may hold autobiographical information, archives, hyperlinks, ways for reader to interact e.g. *View Comments*

- may change every day

- allows comment from and/or collaboration with others

b) Language

- informal and personal e.g. *In my never-ending quest; cool story*

- first person singular and plural e.g. *I came across; we decided to try*

- related to specific topic and purpose of blog e.g. *farming; lambing*

- informative on a specific topic e.g. *radio-controlled drone and a GoPro camera to check on their sheep*

- personal point of view offered

c) Grammar

- present or past tense usually though future possible e.g. *I decided to paint*

- accuracy will depend on ability of writer

- straightforward, conversational language likely

- simple sentence structure

title tells blog's focus

date important as blogs need to be up to date

Go to: Rosie's Education | Go Dairy

HOME

ABOUT ROSIE · MOOVIES · ROSIE'S BLOG
FUN STUFF · ROSIE'S FARM · GALLERY · ROSIE'S CLUB

ASK ROSIE

Rosie's Blog

Home > Rosie's Blog

Rosie's Blog

Recent quad bike to quad-copter!

Posted on Friday, 12 September 2014.

Recent Post

Ben is mooficially bigger than Shrek!
The Moonawatu A&P Show!
Picture Perfect Poetry!
Happy Hallmooween Moo Guys!
Class, calves, and milk from grass!

Archive

2014 November (3)
2014 October (5)
2014 September (4)
2014 August (5)
2014 July (4)
2014 June (4)
2014 May (5)
2014 April (4)
2014 March (5)
2014 February (4)
2014 January (2)
2013 December (4)
2013 November (5)
2013 October (10)
2013 September (8)
2013 August (9)
2013 July (10)
2013 June (9)
2013 May (10)
2013 April (8)
2013 March (10)
2013 February (7)
2013 January (6)

Join Rosie's fan club

image created to match story

friendly tone; personal voice; simple sentence structure

In my never-ending quest to keep up with everything new in the world of farming, I came across a cool story about a farmer and his son on the South Island who are using a radio-controlled drone and a GoPro camera to check on their sheep during lambing. What usually takes them 2 hours on a quad bike only takes them 20 minutes with the drone. I showed the article to my farmer, and we decided to try the same thing on our dairy farm in Raglan.

humour

exclamation mark to suggest tone

I've also been doing some research lately on bees for an upcoming project of mine, which you'll find out about in a few weeks. While doing my research I found out that male bees are called drones as well, so I decided to paint our radio-controlled drone to look like a bee. If you're around Raglan and you happen to see what looks like a giant bee in the sky, don't worry because neither type of drone has a stinger!

Top ^

View Comments (4)

Improve Your Vocabulary

adversarial: an adversary is an enemy. Language that is adversarial excludes someone; creates an 'us and them' situation.

alliteration: the repetition of consonant sounds, especially in poetry

angle: point of view

anomaly: an exception, something that does not fit in

apt: appropriate

authenticity: genuineness, not false or fake

blank verse: verse that doesn't rhyme but has a regular rhythm and metre

byline: the author's name on an article

chronological: according to time sequence, in order

climax: a turning point, the height of a crisis

clincher: a strong concluding sentence or point made in a text

colloquial: everyday, ordinary language

connotation: positive or negative image or word association

context: within a situation, in a specific place or time

emotionally detached: unemotional, cold character or behaviour

expletive: swear word

explicit: clear, definite

figurative language: makes comparisons, uses words for dramatic or poetic effect; opposite of literal language

format: layout, procedure

generic: general, rather than specific, characteristics of something

genre: a synonym for text type

hook: a device to gain the reader's interest

hypothesis: a theory, point of view or angle that is proved in an essay or in writing

imperative: a command or strong advice

inclusive pronoun: such as 'we' and 'our', which includes the reader

irony / ironic: a gap between what is said and what is meant, like sarcasm

literary: refers to writing of a perceived high quality

metaphor: a form of figurative language that compares two objects by saying that one is the other

non-verbal feature: non-speaking gesture such as facial expression or stance

parameter: guideline; the breadth or extent of text

personal referent: reference to the writer to create a closer relationship

personification: to give human qualities to things or animals

primary source: information quoted from an eyewitness

rebuttal: the demolition / rejection of an opponent's argument

reinforce: to strengthen or support

resist: to weaken by disagreement

rhetorical question: a question that does not require an answer

secondary source: information quoted from a text

sentence fragment: incomplete sentence, often used to create a dramatic effect

sibilance: the repetition of an 's' sound, particularly in poetry

signposting: indicating / hinting at the direction a text or story is taking

simile: comparing two objects using the words 'like' or 'as'

subjective: personal as opposed to impersonal; opposite of objective

superlative: adjective denoting the best or the most extreme example of something

terminology: specialist words for a specific subject

testimonial: endorsement by experts

uncluttered: spare in detail, not overdone

validate: to prove

verbal feature: feature of speech such as tone of voice or volume

1. **Advertisement:** Develop your own advertisement for a product aimed at teenagers.

2. **Agenda and Minutes:** Write up the minutes of an imaginary sporting club meeting.

3. **Autobiography / Biography:** Write a chapter of your autobiography about one important stage of your life. Or research the life of a famous person who interests you and write a chapter detailing an important part of his or her life.

4. **Brochure / Flyer:** Create either of these items to market a new product.

5. **Documentary:** View and review a documentary, evaluating its effectiveness as a nonfiction film.

6. **Editorial:** Write an editorial on a controversial issue. Read the newspaper to find a topic.

7. **Essay — Comparative:** Discuss or compare the issues revealed in a feature film and a work of prose fiction.

8. **Essay — Persuasive:** Write a persuasive essay on an issue you feel strongly about.

9. **Feature Article:** As a journalist, write a feature article on a newsworthy item, bringing more depth and background to the subject.

10. **Film Review:** Review a film that you have seen lately either at the cinema, or on TV or DVD.

11. **Job Application — Letter and Résumé:** Write a job application in an area of work that interests you. Add a résumé.

12. **Job Interview:** Now write an imaginary interview in which you demonstrate your aptitude for the job above.

13. **Letter — Business:** Write a business letter of complaint about a faulty product.

14. **Letter to the Editor:** Write a persuasive letter to the editor on an issue you feel strongly about.

15. **Narrative Genres:** Choose one of the narrative genres modelled earlier in the book and write a story conforming to the guidelines for that genre.

16. **News Article:** Write a news article on a topic that interests you — real or imaginary.

17. **Nonfiction:** Write a nonfiction article based on something you have learnt in Science or Geography class.

18. **Novel Essay:** Write an analytical essay on a novel that you have read recently. Analyse the issues in a novel you are studying in class.

19. **Online Texts:** Create your own homepage or blog on a special subject.

20. **Play Essay:** How entertaining is a drama you have seen, read or studied in class? Does it persuade you to a particular point of view?

21. **Play Review:** Read or view a play and write a review of it.

22. **Play Script:** Create a play script from your imagination or turn a chapter of a novel, a short story, or a film or TV programme into a play script.

23. **Poetry Essay:** Choose a poem you particularly like, or your own poem, and write a short analytical essay about it.

24. **Report:** Isolate a problem in your community or in society as a whole. Do some research and present your findings in report format.

25. **Research Assignment and Reference List:** Choose a historical era or an environmental topic that interests you, develop a hypothesis and write up a referenced assignment with a correctly set out reference list.

26. **Shakespearean Drama:** Find a famous speech from a Shakespearean play. Learn it off by heart. Then analyse its meaning and its blank verse.

27. **Shakespearean Essay:** Write an analytical essay on an aspect of the Shakespearean play that you are studying.

28. **Short Story:** Write a short story with a twist.

29. **Song:** Compose your own song.

30. **Speech:** Write a speech to be delivered on an important social occasion.

31. **Textual Intervention:** Write a prelude, interlude or postlude chapter to add to the novel that you are studying.

32. **Textual Reconstruction:** Use the novel as a starting point to change some aspect of the novel you are studying.

Table of Text Types

Creative	Informative	Literary	Media	Persuasive	Spoken
• Autobiography / Biography • Narrative Genre: – teenage romance – contemporary novel • Play Script: – writing and performing • Short story • Song • Textual Intervention • Textual Reconstruction	• Agenda and Minutes • Letter: business • Autobiography / biography • Nonfiction • Novel – essay • Short story • Play: – essay – review • Shakespearean drama • Documentary • Report • Essay: – comparative – persuasive • Poetry Essay • Feature Article • News Article • Film Review • Job Application: – letter – résumé • Job Interview • Research Assignment • Reference list • Speech: – occasional – persuasive • Website: – homepage – blog	• Essay: comparative • Nonfiction • Novel: essay • Poetry: essay • Play: – drama essay – script – Shakespearean drama: essay; analysis • Short story • Textual Reconstruction	• Advertisement • Brochure / Flyer • Documentary • Editorial • News Article • Feature Article • Letter to the Editor • Film Review • Play Review • Website: – homepage – blog	• Advertisement • Brochure / Flyer • Editorial • Letter to the Editor • Essay: persuasive • Speech: persuasive • Film Review • Play Review • Job Application letter • Job Interview • Research Assignment • Website: – homepage – blog	• Job Interview • Speech: – occasional – persuasive • Writing and performing a play script

The person who constructed this poem was having fun. It is made up of lines from famous poems and rhymes. You will recognise some immediately. Use the internet to find those you do not know.

Why waste your time reading lots of poems when one poem has it all?!
(Please note the irony used here.)

The Essential Poem

I wandered lonely as a cloud,
To the lonely sea and sky,
The noblest Roman of them all,
Will know the reason why.

There's a breathless hush in the close tonight,
Cap'n, art tha sleeping there below?
"The time has come," the walrus said,
"I will arise and go."

She walks in beauty like the night,
With sixty seconds' worth of distance run.
The woods are lovely, dark and deep,
Her eyes are nothing like the sun.

April is the cruelest month,
When icicles hang by the wall,
A man's a man for a' that,
Old Uncle Tom Cobley and all.

The king was in his counting house,
Drinking the blood-red wine,
The ploughman homeward plods his weary way,
O World! O Life! O Time!

For east is east and west is west,
Nor all that glisters gold,
Should auld acquaintance be forgot,
In the brave days of old?
